ES Believers
"Plus"

by Vic DaPra
& David Plues

ISBN 978-1-57424-419-9
SAN 683-8022

Design - David Plues & Vic DaPra

Thank You

The "Special Merit" award for ES Believers goes to Joe Bonamassa for his support throughout the series and for writing the foreword for this edition. Also, Rick Gould his photographer and guitar curator for providing great shots of the guitars

Special thanks to Albert Molinaro, Dave Hinson and Drew Berlin who, once again, added so much to the book.

Special mention to Derek Bruneau, Jacques Menache Masri, Keith Milne, Nino Fazio and Simon Gauf who provided stunning photographs. All of the submissions were of the highest standard and we thank each and every one of you for your dedication and shared passion.

Following on from our Burst and Goldtop Believers books we now turn our thoughts to the wonderful ES models which helped shape modern music in the '50s and '60s and are still the favoured instrument for many musicians. The introduction of the thin-line models created a legion of fans looking for an alternative to deep jazz bodies or solid guitars. Huge tonal range could be achieved with the center-block designed guitars which were introduced to reduce feedback and increase sustain. The ES-175 is Gibson's longest-running model and is still in production with the 335 the most successful of the range. A late-'50s early '60s 335 PAF equipped guitar is one of the most sought-after instruments on the planet. Joe Bonamassa says it all in the foreword to this book.

Photo credit for the main cover - Albert Molinaro
1961 Cherry ES-335 Serial # 9898

ES Believers
"Plus"

Thanks to our friend Ron Middlebrook at Centerstream and the dedicated people at Hal Leonard for their support with the series.

Thomas Tull, Joe Bonamassa, Alex Lifeson, Martin Taylor, Eric Johnson, Chris Cain, Peter Frampton, Jorma Kaukonen, Larry Carlton, Elvin Bishop, Kirk Fletcher, Bernie Marsden, Barrie Cadogan, Gene Cornish, Eric Clapton, Rusty Anderson, Elliot Easton, Tom Bukovac, Ford Thurston, Warren Haynes, Howard Leese, G E Smith, Steve Howe, Keith Richards, Dave Edmunds, Mick Moody, Justin Hayward, Ritchie Blackmore, Cosmo, Alvin Lee, Jeff Beck, Ted Nugent, Joe Brown, Val McCallum, Alan Darby, B.B. King, Sonny Burgess, Chuck Berry, Ray Ennis

We could not have produced this book without the great help from the "Believer" friends - thanks to:

Clive Wisbey, Andy Cesarini, Willie Smith, Jan Zander, Dave Brewis, Raul Barrios, Jonas Stanley, Tom Wilson, Rick Hogue, Brent Coleman, Bob Wootton, Cal Wootton, Lou Gatanas, Paul Hamwijk, Mike Slubowski, Koji Shimada, Dag Lutyen, Matt Swanson, Chris Soucy, Bill Fajen, Dave Keeling, Bruce Sandler, Charlie Gelber, John Ladas, John Ducci, Trey Rabinek, Zac Arch, Binky Philips, Carter Vintage, Rich Taylor, Roberto Gandolfi, Andy Shapiro, Matt Walton, Ricky Steel Edge, Masa Hatta, Tobin Dale, Keith Gregory, Leon Windleband, Hiroshi Inoue, Elton Ko, Tobi Kunze, Lee Vincent Grubb, Zac Oswald, Robert Bergeron, Joel Peter Willing, Andy Watts, Francesco Ballosino, Alex Pavchinski, Paul Drenan, Brad Dudley, Mirlado Vidal, Ram Rujinarong, T.J.Smith, Amedeo Riccioni, James Lubbard, Hanks Vintage Guitars, Ray Pinglora, Paul Binotto, Max Crace, Suzy Tyler, Lisa Jenkins, John McIntosh, Vanessa Kaukonen, Robert S Williams, Jon Roncolato, Gary Dick, Tom Wittrock, Duncan Findlay, Dekel Bor, Michael Eaton, Richard Sibbald, Nick Bedessem, Stefano Tonicello, Alex Polata, Roberta Cadore, John Chin, Rob Arthur, Micahael McLuhan, Ben Brion, Rodolphe Bricard. Bill Bernstein, Judy Totton, Tamarind Free Jones, John Taylor, Charlie Daughtry, Ken Settle, Martyn Turner, Tadahiko Okazaki, Jay Rosen,Steve Gornall, Barney Roach, Giovana Pili, Ben Isaacs, Chris Marksbury, M J Kim, Wennan Sun, Michael Zaporozhets, Re-caster, Bill Townsend, Leon Hastwell, Werner Goertz, Daniel Valledor, Helmi Flick, Glen A Gross, Masha Vesset, Martin Lavallée

FOREWORD - JOE BONAMASSA

The Gibson ES (Electric Spanish) series, which originally included the ES-330, ES-335, ES-345 and ES-355 models were a groundbreaking set of guitars designed by Gibson circa 1958 and 1959 by pioneering guitar executive/designer Ted McCarty. I believe they launched these as part of Gibson's modernization campaign which started in 1958 and included other iconic designs like the Flying V, Futura and Moderne.

Whenever I think of ES guitars, one historic example always pops to mind from the movie "Back to the Future." While some might point out that Michael J. Fox played a red 345 at a high school dance in 1955 - a full three years before they officially came out - most of us know better. I suppose Doc Brown may have truly caused a material change in the space-time continuum but it seems unlikely. However, if you believe what you see in the movies, it will remain one of the great mysteries of guitar history. For now, let's not argue about that and just agree to allow this isolated case of movie folklore to remain "unsolved."

So with that said, what is it that makes folks gravitate to the Electric Spanish series? In my opinion it is the guitars sonic versatility, playability, and frankly, its good looks that makes them so popular. Every time I saw someone playing an ES guitar I knew this must be a real serious musician. From iconic jazz players to hard rock superheroes the ES series has produced a wide variety of guitar tones that upon first hearing might be credited to its blood relatives within the Gibson brand like the Les Paul Standard and Custom. I wanted a walnut-colored 355 because of BB in Zaire and I wanted a red one cause of Freddie at the Cotton Bowl. I wanted a '64 cherry 335 because of Eric at the The Albert Hall in 1968 and wanted a red 345 because of Elvin Bishop. This was the music of my youth and the guitars these gentlemen played were sexy and demanded attention. These are the tones I grew up idolizing and longing to achieve.

When you stop long enough to think about it, the ES series guitars are responsible for some of the greatest electric guitar tones Gibson has ever produced. Whether it be "Cliffs of Dover" by Eric Johnson (yes you heard me right), "Live at the Regal" B.B. King, Cream's "Crossroads" at Winterland, or Larry Carlton on "Kid Charlemagne," that warm human voice sound permeates regardless of the player or style. I remember playing Alvin Lee's 1960 dot-neck 335 at the Royal Albert Hall in London. It was a magical experience. I can see why a player like Alvin loved that guitar so much. It gave back what you gave it. It is a wonderful iconic instrument that I feel blessed to have used once...especially in that setting. Bottom line is that you can get a big sound at a big volume all the while retaining that signature f-hole based hollow body sound. The feeling of the body vibrating against your chest when you're playing at feedback volume is unlike any other electric guitar. I know why these have come to be known as the "Stradavarius of Gibson electrics."

Now, the word on the street is that late '50s dot necks are Sunburst Les Paul killers. I agree...and the reality is that as prices steadily increase that you might wake up one morning and see a $200,000 dollar blonde Dot from 1959 with a sold sign on it. The days of ES guitars being "gateway drugs" for players and collectors until they can afford a vintage PAF gold top or sunburst are (in my opinion) coming to an end. The word is out.

When my friends show up at a gig, they always compliment the sound of my vintage Les Pauls but invariably point out that my red 1963 ES-335 or the 1964 ES-355 mono steal the show. A good ES will always be a star in anyone's studio and gig arsenals. One of the best pieces of advice I could give anyone is not to listen with your eyes and don't listen to the internet chatter saying the only magic was contained in the earliest PAF-equipped examples. A late 60s early 70s ES guitar is a truly wonderful instrument. Good enough for Larry and good enough for me. Nobody should be afraid of a slim-taper nut. It is also the opinion of this writer that the ES line of modern day Gibson is the finest that company has produced since the golden era of the late 50's. Their construction and playability are wonderful at a fraction of the price of a vintage model. There are many options at all price points and I whole-heartedly advise that you venture into this territory.

To sum it up, this book showcases the beauty and wonder of the vintage ES guitars and I hope you enjoy exploring its pages as I have.

Thank you Vic for honoring me with this task and for your friendship over these past 20 years. I am sure this will be another winner in a long standing series of great books for true "Believers."

Cheers

Joe Bonamassa

This group of 1959 ES models includes the rare first Blond
ES-355 produced by Gibson.

1936 ES-150
4400 3 (FON)

The Gibson ES (Electric-Spanish) 150, commonly referred to as "The Charlie Christian Model," was introduced in 1936 and started the ES series line of guitars.

Photo credit: Giovana Pili
Thanks to Jacques Menache Masri

Charlie Christian

9

1950 ES-5

1951 L-5 SEC (CES)
A-8821

Note the black bakelite switch-tip which came only with the
earliest ones. The guitar has "SEC" on the label, instead of CES, and
the hyphen after the A in the serial number.

Nino Fazio - Messina Italy

1949 ES-125 T

A9973

Bonnie Raitt

Photo credit: Albert Molinaro

1953 ES-295
A13578

Thanks to Andrea Cesarini

18

1953 ES-350
A 15791

Thanks to Rick Hogue and Nick Bedessem
Garrett Park Guitars

1955 ES-295 SONNY BURGESS
A21351

September 28, 2002

To whom it may concern;

This 1955 Gibson ES295 Guitar serial number A21351 was purchased new by me at Vandyke furniture in Newport Arkansas. It was used for various live performances, photos, and recordings including the 1956 Sun Record Release "Red Headed Woman". This guitar was later traded in at Vandyke furniture for a Fender guitar in 1956.

Sincerely,

Sonny Burgess

Sonny Burgess

Sworn before me this 28 day of Sep.

Donna Rutledge
Notary Public

DONNA RUTLEDGE
Pulaski County
My Commission Expires
September 4, 2011

Thanks to RJ for this feature

Sonny Burgess, Sun Records Gibson ES-295 epitomizes Rock & Roll and is the first status symbol for the first Rock-a-Billy guitar. In 1954 Sonny Burgess got advice from record producer Sam Phillips, to form a group which expanded to Sonny Burgess and the Pacers. The band's first record was "We Wanna Boogie" in 1956 for Sun Records, in Memphis. The flip side was "Red Headed Woman." Both songs were written by Burgess. Sonny Burgess's songs have been described by Rolling Stone Magazine as "among the most raucous, energy-filled recordings released during the first flowering of rock and roll." Sonny Burgess and the Pacers onstage antics in performance were similarly described. Like other artists such as Ray Harris, Hayden Thompson, Billy Lee Riley, and Warren Smith, Sonny Burgess had chart success with "We Wanna Boogie" and "Red Headed Woman." Burgess disbanded the group in 1971 but later found a new audience in Europe. Burgess was inducted into the Rock and Roll Hall of Fame of Europe in 1999. His group, now called "The Legendary Pacers," was a hit that same year in a rockabilly concert in Las Vegas, Nevada.

Sonny Burgess's original Gibson ES-295 guitar is the guitar used at Sun Records by Sonny Burgess, on the hit records "We Wanna Boogie" and "Red Headed Woman" and many other Sun Records. The ultimate classic Rock-a-Billy guitar, from one of the original founders of rock & roll. The guitar is just like Scotty Moore's Gibson ES-295 guitar used at Sun Records with Elvis in the early 1950s. These 2 guitars are the first used that started the first flowering of Rock and Roll. Sonny is epitomized as the quintessential, original, one and only first real Rock-a-Billy Kat.

1955 ES-350 N

Tatanka Guitars Collection
Photo credit: Stefano Tonicello

CHUCK BERRY

The Gibson P-90 equipped ES-350 N is one of the most historically important guitars in rock and roll history. Chuck Berry, nicknamed "The Father of Rock & Roll" played this model on his breakthrough smash hits "Maybelline" and "Roll Over Beethoven."

With guitar in hand and his famous "duck walk," he shook the world when he performed on The Dick Clark Show.

1956 ES-295

A 23914

Scotty Moore was a true innovator and a rock and roll pioneer. He is shown here with Elvis in this 1950s photo playing his Gibson ES-295

26

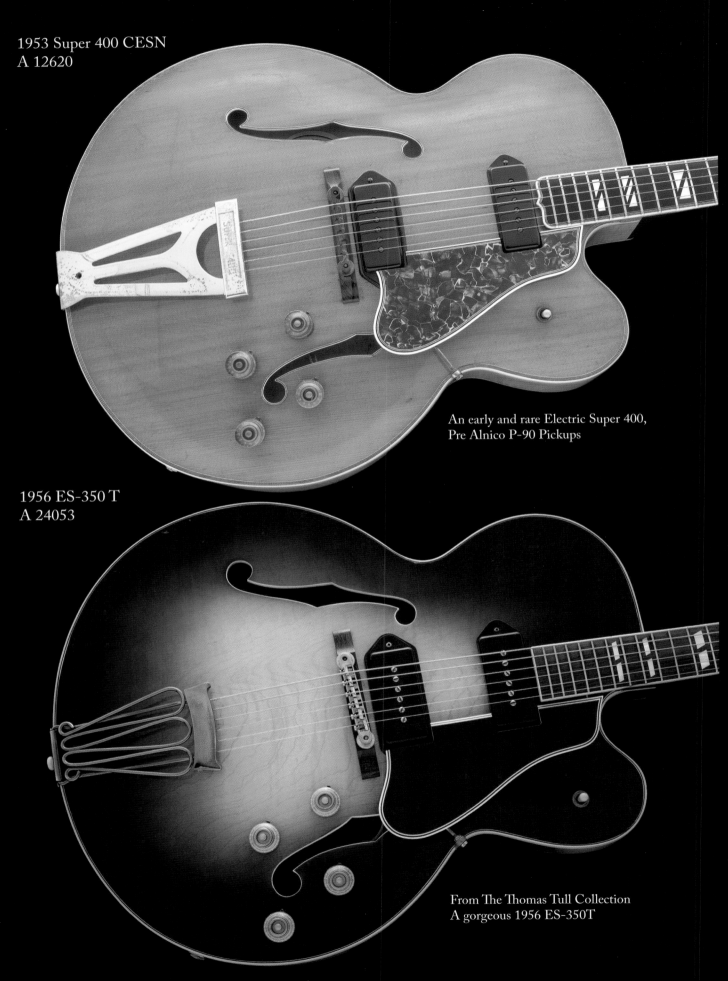

1953 Super 400 CESN
A 12620

An early and rare Electric Super 400,
Pre Alnico P-90 Pickups

1956 ES-350 T
A 24053

From The Thomas Tull Collection
A gorgeous 1956 ES-350T

1957 Byrdland
A 25999

1968 L5 CESN, Sharp Cut
515917

From The Thomas Tull Collection. A very pretty 1957
Byrdland with Alnico P-90's

Photography by Albert Molinaro

1957 GIBSON ES175
BLONDE
26239

1954 GIBSON ES175
BLONDE
17882

Owned by Brent Coleman, photographed by Derek Bruneau

Submitted by: Nino Fazio, Messina Italy

ALEX LIFESON of RUSH

I was 12 years old when I received my first cheap guitar, a $10 acoustic and I played that guitar constantly until the following Christmas when I received my second cheap guitar, a $59 electric semi-hollow body. It was all my parents could afford and I loved that one, but in my dreams, I always pictured a Gibson ES-335. I admired many ES players: Jorma Kaukonen, Alvin Lee, Bob Weir, B.B. King, John Lennon, Eric Clapton and Larry Carlton who all looked so cool to me playing that classically designed semi-acoustic hollow body that has never gone out of fashion since its release in 1958.

It was in the spring of 1969 that I got my first ES-335 TD, and I must have played that guitar every day. It served me well through the bar gig era of Rush and I can recall boiling my strings once a week to stretch a bit more clarity out of them; strings were expensive! Once we started touring in the mid '70s, it was my main guitar up until a gig in 1979 when a PA horn slipped its mooring and came crashing down onto the stage right wing and then fell over onto a few of my guitars. The 335 was damaged on the headstock as well as a deep gouge along the neck. I retired that guitar until the last couple of tours when it reappeared for the encore, Working Man.

In 1976, I took delivery of the ES-355 I affectionately called "Whitey" for its white finish and in honour of our bus driver, Tom "Whitey" Whittaker. That guitar was so much a part of me and my tone, particularly from the mid 1970s through the 1990s before I started carrying more guitars than I could actually play! The tone on that guitar was thicker than the 335s due to the large central body support and tighter fit. I used to stuff cotton batting in through the F holes to make the body slightly less resonant back when my amps were set to 12 to minimize some feedback. It worked somewhat but I think I convinced myself through stubborn belief rather than science. This was also the Norlin era of ownership when Gibson experienced some challenges. The neck was very delicate, narrow and thin. My young 1970s fingers loved it but it became more of a task to fit my much more mature digits between the frets later on!

Over the years, I've owned more than a dozen ES Gibsons including the hybrid ES-Les Paul Signature, but it was a purchase in 2016 of a beautiful 1958 Tobacco Sunburst ES-335 that holds a prominent place on my guitar wall. I've come a long way since that kid with the cheap guitar and big dreams, but I'm both proud and lucky to have that singular guitar model continue to be my beloved inspiration.

Alex

Alex is shown here with his Gibson ES Les Paul Signature Model

Photo credit: Richard Sibbald

We wish to thank John McIntosh for making this feature possible.

Photo credit: Andrew MacNaughtan

Alex Lifeson Vintage ES models

1958 ES-335 TD
A28083

1960 ES-335 TD
R 7436

1961 ES-335 TD
9808

1968 ES-335 TD
120189

Photo credit: Richard Sibbald

1958 ES–175
A 28646

In June 2019, I visited the Songbirds Museum and was particularly drawn to a pristine ES-175 which I had always dreamed of owning, due to my love for Joe Pass, Jim Hall, and Pat Metheny. Three years later, Rick from Garrett Park Guitars posted the self-same guitar for sale. I immediately purchased it, traveling from Brazil to the US to pick it up.

Alessandro Polato

Thanks to Alex Polata for this feature
Photo credit: Roberta Cadore

Val McCallum

1958 ES-335 Dot Neck
A 28761

Val McCallum performing in 2023 with Jackshit band member, drummer, Pete Thomas. Photo credit: John Chin

Whether or not you've heard of Val McCallum, you've undoubtedly heard his work. Val is a supremely talented guitarist, singer, songwriter and studio musician who got his start recording for the legendary songwriter Harry Nilsson at age 18. Over the past 30 years, he went on to work with such artists as Jackson Browne, Lucinda Williams, The Wallflowers, Shelby Lynne, Gregg Allman and countless others. Val started releasing his own solo records, "At the End of the Day" in 2012, "Chateauguay" in 2019, and "Beau Bow de Lune" in 2021, which he co-wrote with songwriter Bow Thayer. Val also co-wrote the rocking song "Cleveland Heart" with Jackson Browne who released it in 2021 as a single. Additionally, Val is well-known as guitarist "Beaushit" and is part of the very popular Los Angeles band called "Jackshit."

Albert Molinaro

When I was a teenager growing up in the 70s, all of my favorite studio guys played ES-335s. Those players included Robben Ford, Lee Rittenour, Jay Graydon and my favorite of all, Larry Carlton. I used to see him at the famous Baked Potato club on a regular basis. Larry's touch, sound and chops were as good as it gets. The ES-335 is the perfect guitar to cover all bases. The more you play one, the more you realize it's all in there. It can rock as hard as a Les Paul— if not more—and by manipulating the controls, can sound beautifully articulate and single-coil-like, too. If I was (God forbid) forced to play only one instrument, it would probably be an ES-335.

Val

Thanks to Albert Molinaro for this feature

1958 ES-350 N
A 29345
with added varitone switch

Owned by Brent Coleman, photographed by Derek Bruneau

58 GIBSON ES350
NATURAL
A 29345

MARTIN TAYLOR MBE

Martin Taylor began his recording career in 1979 working with Ike Issacs on the album "After Hours." This was followed by extensive touring with Stephane Grappelli from 1979 to 1990 occupying the prestigious chair of Django Reinhardt. In 1993, Martin launched his solo career with the groundbreaking solo album "Artistry" (Linn) which was produced by Steve Howe embarking on tours of America, Europe and Asia. In 1996, Martin and Steve Howe recorded the Scott Chinery Guitar Collection and The Blue Guitars Collection on "Masterpiece Guitars" (The Guitar Label). Another notable recording was the award-winning duet album "Tone Poems II" (Acoustic Disc) with David Grisman featuring vintage guitars and mandolins. He now manufactures his own brand of jazz guitar but has great memories of playing 175s and the Johnny Smith model.

"I had a 1964 Gibson ES175 that I bought in New York back in 1973. I never recorded with it and sold it in 1977 to buy a 1970 Gibson Johnny Smith, which I played on my first album "Taylor Made" in 1978. I've also owned, and still own, a 1925 L4 Eddie Lang, and two "A" Style mandolins from 1908 and 1918. My Johnny Smith which was more of an orange/red sunburst rather than the usual antique sunburst. I didn't actually play the JS for very long, maybe only four or five years. I then started to play the WG Barker during my Stephane Grappelli years."

Martin

www.martintaylor.com

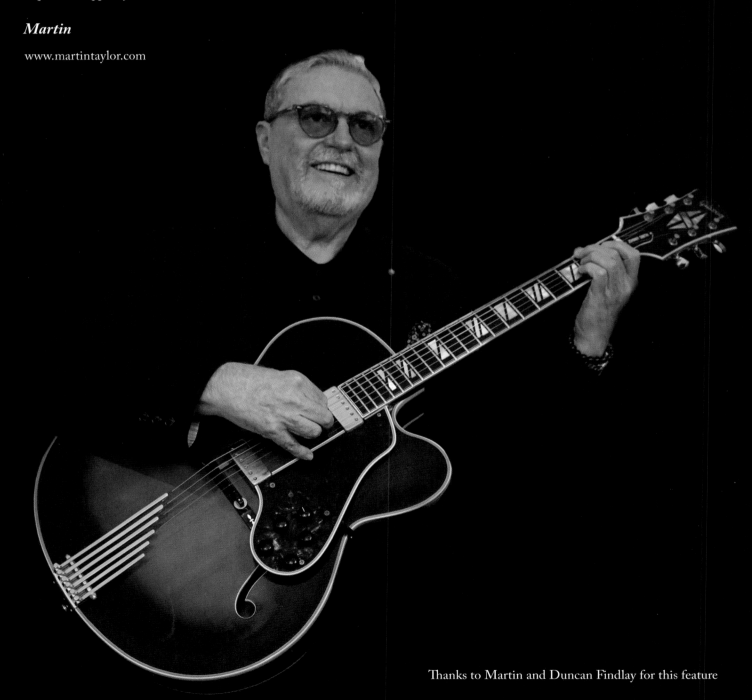

Thanks to Martin and Duncan Findlay for this feature

Johnny Smith

The Gibson Johnny Smith Model. Released in 1961, this guitar held the honour of being Gibson's most expensive artist model, and only less expensive than the Super 400. The Johnny Smith Model was discontinued at the end of 1969.

JOHNNY SMITH

Thanks to Gary Dick

1958 ES-175 D-N
A 27457

The "N" designates a natural finish and "D" means double pickup. This model is on the bottom end of the ES big box guitars, but is definitely one of the more popular models!

ERIC JOHNSON

A friend of mine named Jimmy Schade had a 335. He was one of the people that I learned to play from, and I was attracted to the beauty of the guitar that he had. It was a mid-60s Sunburst one. Soon after, my father helped me acquire a red 335 from the local music store in Austin called JR Reed's Music. I was 13 then, and have loved those guitars ever since.

They have a timeless beauty about them, and they are a wonderful musical negotiation between all styles of music. They are probably my favorite Gibson guitar made, and each one of them has a magic uniqueness to it. You can get quite addicted to the acoustical nature of them, as opposed to a solid-body guitar sometimes.

To me, along with the Stratocaster, it is the most quintessential and important guitar of my musical journey.

Eric

Thanks to Eric Johnson, Max Grace and Dave Hinson for this feature

1958 ES-335 TDN
A 28558

This particular blond ES-335 has very
stunning Birdseye maple top.

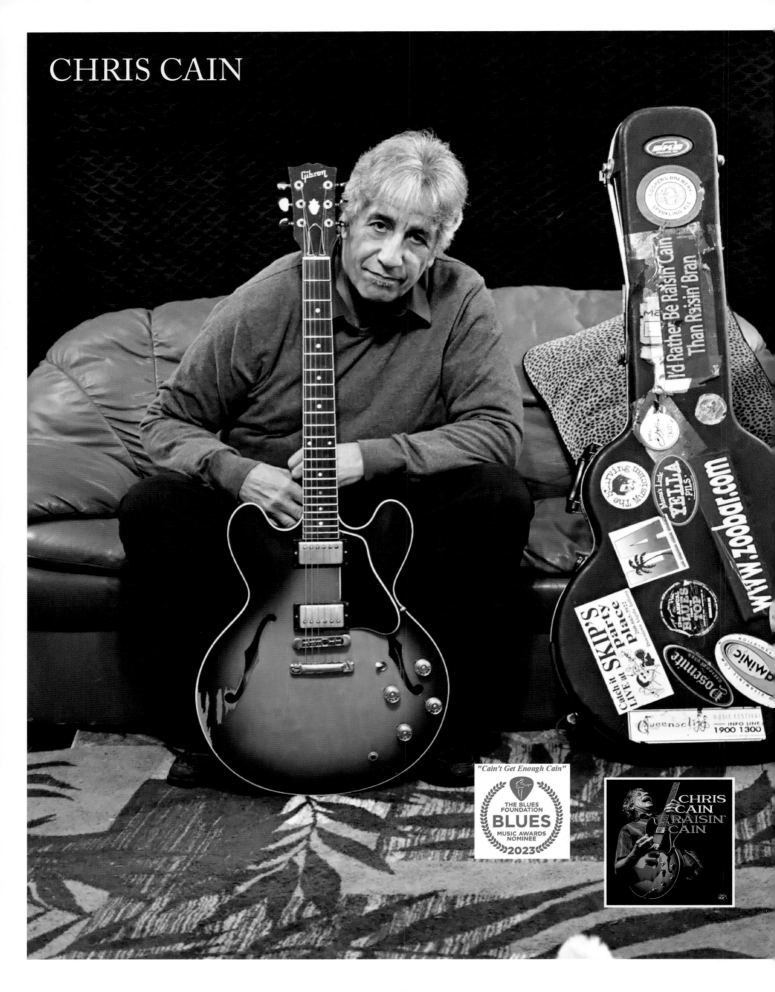

CHRIS CAIN

The 335 was such an incredible looking guitar. The first one I noticed was played by Jerry Newton, Wayne Newton's brother, back when they were a duo in Las Vegas. I saw a short film from their show in one of the lounges on the bar TV. I was really drawn to Sunburst Les Pauls since seeing the Rolling Stones in 1965, but this Gibson looked jazzy like something an older cat would play. I always dug seeing someone with a 335 Sunburst or Cherry. Beautiful. My first lesson was on a SG Standard. My brother Tootie got it for me after hearing how incredible it was millions of times. I played that from 1969 to 1986 about 25 hours a day. I loved it and felt that was it. I had a really incredible Gibson SG but then I saw Robben Ford with the Yellow Jackets and I was absolutely blown out. I had been seeing Robben since 1972 and his L5 was such a beautiful looking guitar through a Bassman, it was life changing. That tone and those incredible ideas. I thought that's all he'd ever need. A classic jazz guitar in his hands, it could make you want to quit. Then, I saw the Yellow Jackets a bunch of times and that 335 he had was magical through the Boogie he used the first time I saw him with his 335. He used Yamahas by the time the second record came out and his playing with that guitar was beyond inspiring.

I couldn't get the look of that guitar out of my mind. It looked perfect. The cutaways, the pickguard and the humbuckings. These things were very expensive. At first, I hadn't considered something like that, but I was playing my SG through a Twin. It was harsh sounding. A sunburst 335 had always been an unobtainable dream but I was lucky enough to find a way to actually buy my 335. I traded a 1970 Les Paul with the little Humbuckers and $350 for a beauty that had been at this Guitar Center since it opened. It was a life-changing day because I bought one of the first Mesa Boogies with three knobs and those two together, 335 and Boogie, changed my playing experience. It was the first time I heard the tone that I could always hear in my head. The greatest looking semi-acoustic electric guitar, in my humble opinion. Her name was Hortense. I loved that guitar. But after having her for five years, Hortense was stolen while I was on tour. It was devastating.

Right around that time, guitarists Terry Holmes and Herb Ellis talked to Gibson and got me an incredible 335. Her name is Melba and she's been with me playing dates ever since. The one they sent had pickups that looked like Humbuckers but you could talk into them like a microphone. Then I heard about a guy whose wife smashed his 335 into a fine powder and I bought the guts from the poor guy and got my Music Man RD112 and have been playing them since my first record. I feel like I know that guitar and she knows me. I have a few other guitars, but Melba is what I have always played, and I am satisfied. I feel blessed to have found the guitar that would end up being my sound, something folks have said they recognise, sometimes, and I say it's that Gibson 335. It is extremely easy to get a lot of different sounds with the same guitar.

I love this Gibson Guitar and feel it's the only one I can play at all.

Chris

Thanks to Susan Tyler and Chris Cain for this feature

1958 ES-355
A 28421

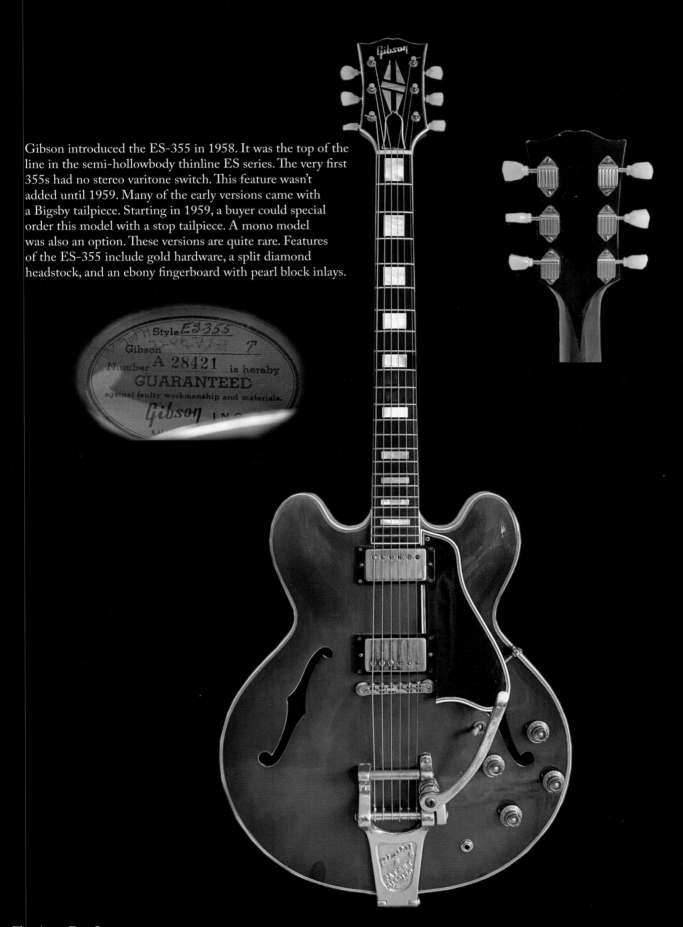

Gibson introduced the ES-355 in 1958. It was the top of the line in the semi-hollowbody thinline ES series. The very first 355s had no stereo varitone switch. This feature wasn't added until 1959. Many of the early versions came with a Bigsby tailpiece. Starting in 1959, a buyer could special order this model with a stop tailpiece. A mono model was also an option. These versions are quite rare. Features of the ES-355 include gold hardware, a split diamond headstock, and an ebony fingerboard with pearl block inlays.

Thanks to Dag Lutyen

PETER FRAMPTON

We would like to thank Peter for his contributions to the "Believer" series of books.

He's been there for us every time we've asked.

When I first started playing guitar, my favourite Gibson was the ES 335. I saw local guitarists playing these lovely sounding and looking guitars I couldn't afford. When I was in the band The Herd, I bought an ES 175. This was because I was listening to lots of jazz guitarists like Kenny Burrell and Wes Montgomery. I instantly loved the beautiful tone of an ES guitar.

It wasn't until much later that I bought my first ES 335. It's a 1964 cherry red guitar that has the tone of Freddy King's brighter sounding 335 guitar. And I believe Eric used one of the same year for Cream's farewell RAH concert. Later, having fallen in love with this style of guitar, I wanted to get another with a different tonal spectrum. I was very lucky to find a 1959 cherry ES 335. Most were sunburst until 1960. But in '59, Gibson was experimenting with different colours. Voila! The signature cherry red 335 was born!

My wish for a slightly different tone was definitely granted. The 1959 ES 335 happens to be the warmest sounding semi-acoustic guitar I own. Oh, and for some reason, the loudest too. It's way louder. If you told me I could only keep one guitar, then this would be the one. There are only a handful of guitar models that can pretty much sound right on any style of music. And to top it all, ES 335s have one of the most beautiful guitar designs ever.

Yep, I'll say it, "They are very sexy looking axes!"

peter frampton

1958 ES-335
A28827

This is a late 1958, 335. The early ones had no binding, a thin Tune-o-matic bridge that usually collapses and would need a filed down normal ABR-1 to compensate for the bad neck angle. This particular model is a late '58 with binding and correct neck angle which accommodates a regular Tune-o-matic.

1958 ES-335

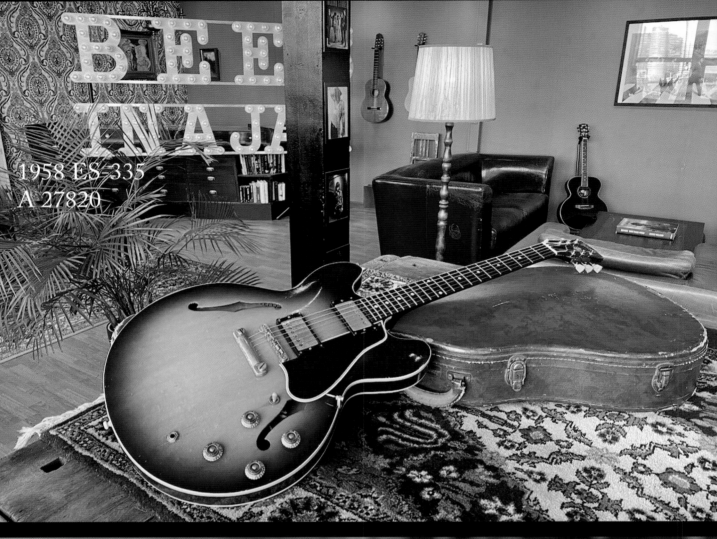

1958 ES-335
A 27820

.Photo credit: Paul Hamwijk

Photo credit: Lou Gatanas

One of the first 335s made. Look where the fingerboard overlaps the body at the highest frets and you will see that it is without the usual white edge binding. Only the earliest examples were without this binding. This 1958 ES-335 has been rumored to be possibly owned by Peter Green

LARRY CARLTON

Larry recently partnered with guitar manufacturer Sire who worked with Larry on the quality and sound of his new line of guitars. Larry always had a concern that those who followed his career would not be able to afford the ES-335. After years of searching, Larry and his manager Robert Williams found the opportunity to work with an incredible company that produces high quality guitars at a reasonable price.

Larry Carlton, Mr. 335, is accepted as the consummate master of tone and invention with the 335. He worked with Steely Dan, The Crusaders and performed on countless recording sessions. The song "Kid Charlemagne" on the album Royal Scam by Steely Dan is one of the highlight songs that truly captures Larry's playing. He continued with a solo career recording at his home studio named Studio 335.

"It's common knowledge that, by luck, my ES-335 sounds better than any we had ever heard in the '70s," says Carlton.

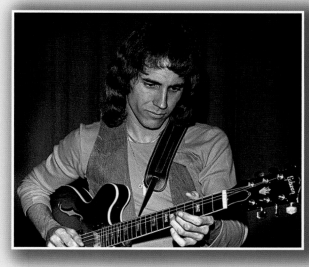

Vintage Mr. 335

Thanks to Larry and Robert S. Williams for this feature

Here is a stunning 1958 ES-335 T. The early guitars have some features that changed shortly after production got into full swing. Some of these features include an unbound fingerboard, a low-height Tune-o-matic bridge to compensate for the early production low neck angle, a long pickguard, a thinner ply top, as well as body construction and body shape changes, these features eventually all changed over time.

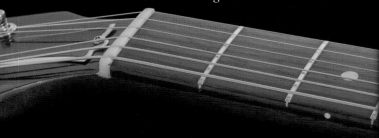

Below photo:
One of the more noticeable features of an early production ES-335 is an Unbound Fingerboard

Left photo:
These guitars had a slightly less than ideal neck angle necessitating a need for a lower Tune-o-matic bridge

Below photo:
Measurements vary, but the early ply tops were approximately 3.5mm thick increasing to about 5mm. You can also see how the F-holes were trimmed by hand, sunburst finishes usually got brown paint

Below photo:
The earliest guitars had a longer pickguard that protruded past the bridge, it was shortened not long after

Guitar, photos and feature by Albert Molinaro / Elite Guitars

Jorma Kaukonen

Jefferson Airplane, Hot Tuna and Rock and Roll Hall of Fame member

My Life & Times With The ES-345
Thursday, April 20, 2023

Yeah, the Gibson ES-345 Stereo, it changed my life in a number of ways. When Paul Kantner first pressed me into service in 1965 into what would become Jefferson Airplane, I had no idea what a true electric guitar had in store for me. At the time I was strictly an acoustic guitar player, although somehow a blond maple 1937 Gibson L-5 had found its way into my possession. It had a DeArmond pickup on it and came with an early 50's Fender Princeton. When I tried out for the band, that's the rig I played. When I passed muster and got into the band, it became immediately apparent that the old L-5 wasn't going to cut it, so I sold it. A story for another time.

Zal Yanovsky of the Lovin' Spoonful was playing a Guild Thunderbird, and the fact that I thought it looked cool outweighed the fact that I wasn't quite sure how to get what I wanted out of it…plus the fact that I didn't really know what I wanted. Indeed, I mean no disrespect to solid body guitars. They have been a major part of my electric guitar arsenal for years. That said, back in those early days I just felt like playing a solid body guitar was, well…cheating in some way.

B.B. King was playing an ES-355. Lots of the Big Dogs I looked up were playing those beautiful guitars. I decided I had to have one. The funny thing at the time was that I didn't realize at the time that the ES-345 was a stereo guitar and what opportunities such a beast would provide. I went down to Sherman & Clay in San Francisco at the corner of Kearny and Sutter. At the time they were mostly a piano store, but they had some guitars as well.

I unloaded the Guild Thunderbird and took the only ES-345 Sherman and Clay had off the wall. It was Cherry Red, of course. It was the most beautiful electric guitar I had ever seen. I can't remember how much it was at the time, probably around five hundred bucks. Whatever it was, I didn't have the money even with my trade in, so I financed it. I was the first thing I ever financed in my life. A big moment for me.

I soon learned that it was a Stereo Guitar with each pickup having its own output…and then there was the Varitone dial and the Bigsby Tailpiece (all gold-plated by the way). So many tonal options. I really had a chance to get to know the guitar when the Airplane was recording After Bathing At Baxters in RCA's Studio A at Sunset and Ivar. I bought two Fender Twins (also from Sherman & Clay) and used one for each pickup. I would use a Thomas Organ Company Crybaby on the bridge pickup and a Maestro Fuzz Tone on the neck pickup. The Bigsby Whammy Bar also became part of my sound at the time.

We didn't have drive pedals back then, and the ES-345's Semi Hollow Body made awesome sustain possible even at only 7 or 8 on the amp. Paul Kantner, Marty Balin, and Grace Slick would throw atypical rock songs at me and that beautiful cherry red stereo would show me what I could do with them. I used the bridge pickup most of the time, but that high, singing tone of the neck pickup with all the treble rolled off through the Maestro was another universe.

I actually used the Varitone dial when recording Baxters, but in combat conditions on the road it was always on number one, which had the fattest sound.

Fast forward to the present. In 2016, Jefferson Airplane was honored by NARAS with a Grammy Lifetime Achievement Award. It was decided that we would play a tune at the ceremony. Mike Volz, who was ramrodding the Gibson Custom shop back then, had the Gibson artisans recreate that 1964 ES-345 which they did…and more. When I got that guitar from Mike, it looked and felt like my original one, which by that time was long gone. It was a tactile flashback and sounded terrific. You can probably find a YouTube clip of that Grammy event.

When Electric Hot Tuna tours today, I play that guitar on stage. Of course, it requires a bus tour so I can bring two amps to maximize the stereo effect. These days I use an Alfonso Hermida Zen Drive into my old Cry Baby Wah for the bridge pickup and another Zen Drive for the neck.

Listen to my lead guitar work on the Airplane's "We Can Be Together" on the Volunteers album.

That's the ES-345 that helped change my guitar life.

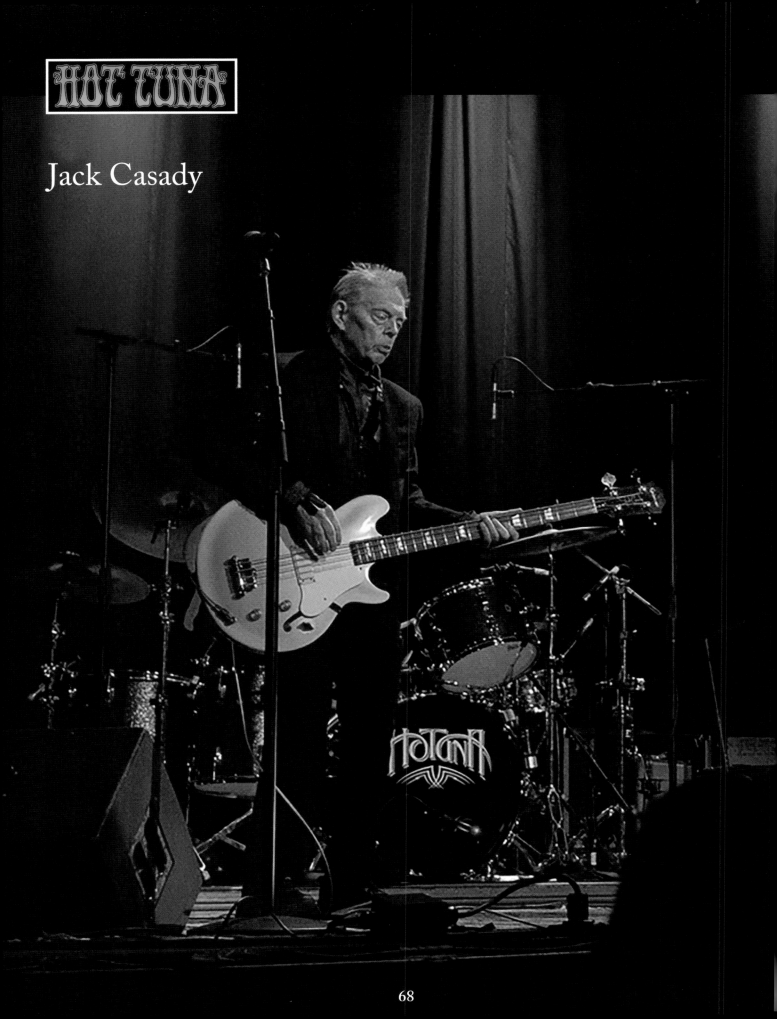

HOT TUNA

Jack Casady

Jorma Kaukonen

Thanks to Vanessa Kaukonen for her assistance with this feature

1959 ES-335 TN
A 30852

ES.335.T	N	A-30852
ES.335.T	N	A 30853
ES.335.T	N	A-3085
S.335.T	N	

Number A 30852 is hereby
GUARANTEED

Thanks to Francesco Balossino

1958 ES-335
A-28362

Left-handed dot necks are quite
rare. It's great to have such a
fine example for this book

1958 ES-5 Switchmaster
A 26940

Photo credit: Mike Slubowski

72

1958 ES-335
A 28110

Photo credit: Koji Shimada

1959 ES 335 SUNBURST
A 33257

A 28110

A short history of the Gibson ES (Electric Spanish) series from the early days to the "Golden Era" of the 1950s and 1960s

Gibson's ES series are possibly some of the most unsung heroes in the history of the electric guitar. An uncanny combination of Gibson's traditional Jazz-box guitars and some "inspiration" from none other than Les Paul, the resultant hybrid of acoustic and electric guitars has, without doubt, had some of the most profound impact on music since its inception than possibly any of its contemporaries. Through their many variations and guises, ES guitars can be seen in the hands of musicians from almost every genre of music, and its widespread reach owes as much to versatility as it does to classic design and timeless quality.

The history of these guitars is a very well-trodden path. In summary, it was the result of the success of Fender's then new-fangled Telecaster (neé Broadcaster). When Fender released the then novel concept of a mass-produced solid bodied guitar, Gibson was certain that it was no more than a passing fad and continued to make instruments for the big band jazz players that they had catered for previously. Enter Les Paul, who some years prior had identified the problem with amplification of these guitars, and brought his "Log" prototype to Gibson—who famously turned him down. The solid centre block and hollow winged design of this "Log" shared a remarkable similarity to what would follow. Fast forward a few years and Fender's Telecaster had proven to be more than a flash in the pan, and by 1954 were on the cusp of releasing a new solid model guitar (the infinitely popular and iconic Stratocaster). Gibson had of course released the Les Paul model guitar in 1952 to try and cut into this new market—but had yet to really understand what was happening to music at the time. Rock and Roll was quickly becoming the flavour of the day, and Gibson and Les Paul's vision for their solid guitar didn't quite fit into their picture of what their guitars should be. By 1955, the cheaper Les Paul Jr. had become Gibson's top seller, and rivalled their long-standing bestselling model, the ES-125 (introduced in 1937 as the ES-150, famous as the "Charlie Christian" model). This perfectly encapsulates Gibson's dilemma at the time: the clash between old and new. Solid bodied guitars were selling, and they had to compete with their market rivals, who had emerged on the scene after the war with no baggage to hold them back. However, Gibson had heritage, a legacy to uphold, and many musicians placed their trust in Gibson's premium quality instruments.

The original "Electric Spanish" guitars (ES) after the ES-150/125 were the iconic and innovative ES-175, and the ES-5 "Switchmaster," introduced in 1949. These were Gibson's first true experiments in electric acoustic guitar design and were immediately very well received. The ES-175 in particular became somewhat of a cult classic, remaining in production until as recently as 2019, and selling over 37,000 units from '49-'99. These guitars were swiftly succeeded by many new model numbers and variations thereof (all with different prefixes and suffixes, just to keep life confusing- for example, the ES-175 originally featured a single P-90 pickup, however in 1953 they introduced a 2-pickup model entitled the ES-175D for Double Pickup, followed by T for Thinline, C for Cutaway, etc.) such as the ES-140, ES-130, ES-135 and ES-295, and SEC/CES (Cutaway Electric Spanish) series, which were previously popular jazz-box guitars such as the L5 and Super 400 with electronics and pickups installed.

Chuck Berry

These guitars all had something in common, they shared the same construction methods that all of Gibson's post-war arch top guitars featured, which is to say a large hollow body made of laminated maple. According to Ted McCarty, Gibson's famed Golden Age President, "We didn't need all that big body, so we reduced the size of the rim and made it a stronger instrument as far as the structure was concerned. I can't recall where the thinking came from…" A good guess would be the ensuing feedback and hum issues that occurred because of increasingly louder amplifiers and single coil P-90 equipped guitars, and the uncomfortable thickness of such a deep body. It is here that the classic "Thinline" hollow body guitars first came into being in 1955, with the ES-225T, the Byrdland, and followed closely by the ES-350T and with it, the Rock 'n' Roll stylings of a certain Chuck Berry! These new Thinline guitars had a body depth of under two inches, within a few hairs of its best-selling Les Paul Junior model, they proved to be immensely popular indeed and even more ES models followed in 1956. The Les Paul model was still selling well, however many musicians found them to be too heavy and too small to be practical, and so preferred the larger Thinline models. Naturally, they also found usage among the jazz and big band players of the day, Joe Pass, Wes Montgomery, Django Reinhardt, Herb Ellis, and others came to use these guitars at certain points in their careers. So much so that by the late fifties and early sixties some of the models had been named after famous musicians. In a few instances, collaboration between Gibson and the artists resulted in some of the first "signature" models such as Tal Farlow, Barney Kessel, and Johnny Smith.

Despite the popularity of the Thinline however, there was a tonality and sustain inherent to the solid guitar that was becoming increasingly desirable. In 1958, in an effort to combine the Thinline and the solid body, Gibson hit on what would become one of the all-time classics in guitar design, the ES-335. McCarty goes on to say, "The thought was to make a guitar with hollow wings but a solid centre. So, what we did was, take a solid block of maple and run it all the way through the centre of the body. So, you got all the sustain of a solid body with the appearance of a standard guitar." These design changes to the construction of the guitar not only enhanced the tonal characteristics, but lessened the effects of feedback further still—with the additions of spruce fillets underneath the laminated maple arch-back and front to isolate the hollow chambers in each wing. Combined with a new double cutaway shape that gave access to the highest frets comfortably—a design feature that would be carried through into many of Gibson's later models—the most obvious being the "Les Paul Mark II" in 1961 (the SG by any other name) but also the Firebird, and the redesigned Special and Junior models of the early sixties.

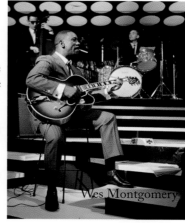
Wes Montgomery

The ES-335 also had to its advantage the fettling that had been done to its solid body older brother over the previous six years. As readers of these books will no doubt be aware, 1958 was the first year in which the Les Paul appeared in its most widely appreciated format: the Sunburst. With its double set of humbucking PAF pickups, and featuring the relatively new Tune-o-matic bridge system, what took the Les Paul model six years to get right allowed the 335 to appear fully-formed, right out of the box—it is no surprise that its basic shape and construction have remained nearly untouched for 65 years. Along with the appearance of the 335, true to form, Gibson released other models with varying specs over the course of 1958 and '59, such as the ES-355, which featured factory-fitted Bigsby vibratos and block inlays, the ES-345 with split parallelogram inlays, the infamous "varitone" circuit (which was also offered on the 335 models of 1959) and stereo output. The ES-345 is probably most famous for its usage in the *Back to the Future* films, as the guitar Marty McFly wields to devastating effect on his decidedly anachronistic rendition of "Johnny B. Goode," resulting in the famous piece of film trivia that not only was the song anachronistic, for being set in 1955 but the guitar itself wasn't manufactured until 1959! The reason for this is that like many films produced around that time, the guitars featured were from the collection of a certain Norm Harris of Norm's Rare Guitars (Nigel Tufnel's guitar room in Spinal Tap is another that springs to mind as being furnished by Norm) and despite Norm's advice into what would have been era appropriate, the director instead insisted that the guitar must be red!

Freddie King

Johnny Rivers

Lesser-known variants were also produced from the late 50's through to the early 60's, such as the ES-330 in 1959 which featured a non-centre block design and a neck set further into the body, the EB-2 bass in 1958 and two years later, a six-string baritone version called the EB-6. 1964 saw the introduction of two more signature guitars to the catalogue, bearing the moniker of Latin-pop star Trini Lopez, one featuring the pointed Venetian style cutaways (similar to the previously mentioned Barney Kessel model) and a more conventional 335 shaped version. Both featured Diamond F-holes and inlays, and a six-aside headstock design—a radical design move from Gibson, who until then had favoured three-aside headstocks almost exclusively. From 1965, Gibson started to produce 12-string 335s, 12-strings being something that was unusual from Gibson. This was a response to the popularity of 12-string models from other manufactures such as Rickenbacker and Gretsch, which found favour among artists like The Beatles and The Monkees. Frank Allen from the English Merseybeat band The Searchers used one such example of a 12-string ES-335. Ironically, Gretsch had started producing double cutaway guitars in the early 60's in retaliation to Gibson's success with the ES-335, showing the tit-for-tat thinking that was going on between the various guitar brands at the time. Even Fender went off-piste and released their 335-inspired Coronado in 1966. Many other smaller manufacturers were to get in on the semi-hollow craze, particularly notable are brands such as Kay and Hofner, who were producing guitars (such as the Hofner Verithin) for the European market, due to the post-war trade embargo which ended in 1959, which made American guitars difficult to obtain and expensive.

In 1957, Gibson acquired the Epiphone brand. Epiphone had been making electric instruments since the 1930s, however, after the acquisition, production turned from the more traditional big-box archtop acoustic designs towards the Thinline designs, in parallel to what Gibson was doing with its own named instruments. Epiphone started to produce guitars such as the Sheraton, Riviera, and Casino models, which were all based on the ES-335 outline, although the Casino was a fully hollow-bodied instrument. Some of the older catalogue models were still produced after the switch, such as the Emperor and Broadway, but the majority were (much the same as today) equivalents to Gibson models, such as the Sorento (ES-125TD) the Granada (ES-120T) and the previously mentioned Sheratons, Rivieras and Casinos which were 335's and 330's respectively. Notable changes include pearl and abalone inlays, floral headstock motifs, "Frequensator" style tailpieces and new, smaller mini-humbucker pickups. Close association with big name artists of the day including The Beatles, Brian Jones and Keith Richards of The Rolling Stones, Ray and Dave Davies of The Kinks, and Pete Townsend of The Who made the Epiphone models exceedingly popular, rivalling their Gibson counterparts.

The lasting appeal of these instruments spans across nearly 80 years and more different genres than can be practically listed. The reasons why are not secret either—with all the different models there truly is something for everyone, and the versatility of these guitars is the stuff of legends. Their comparative underdog status as compared to electric giants such as Les Pauls, Strat's and Tele's however, has seen many of the lesser-known ES models discontinued as part of Gibson's production catalogue, however the heart of the range, the classic 335 (and its variants) have remained a constant presence over the last 70 years of Gibson's history. This fact is exemplified by the long and varied list of notable patrons, and the sheer differences between applications across all musical genres is genuinely remarkable. As would be obvious from its lineage, many jazz players were amongst the first to take up the ES guitars, but they quickly saw usage by early Rock 'n' Roll and Rockabilly pioneers. Scotty Moore, Carl Perkins, and Roy Orbison all famously used ES-175's and 335's respectively. There was also a large uptake amongst blues musicians. Obviously, B.B. King was famous for his almost exclusive use of various 335s and 355s named Lucille, to remember a fire that he narrowly escaped from, which was started by two men fighting over a woman called Lucille, but Freddie King also played a cherry red 355 for most of his later life, after switching out his Gold Top Les Paul. Joined by the likes of T-bone Walker, Lowell Fulson, Otis Rush and John Lee Hooker, the ES guitars became a staple of electric blues music. It is no wonder then, that along with the Les Paul, the guitars that the British Blues players sought out were ES guitars, mainly 335s. The most famous of all of these is of course Eric Clapton, who purchased a new ES-335 in 1964, while he was playing in The Yardbirds. In 2004, when Clapton came to sell this guitar in the Crossroads auction, in the catalogue he states: "This is the second electric guitar I bought. I had a pinky red Telecaster, and then this...I bought this brand new, either from Denmark Street or Charing Cross Road...I went and bought [this] guitar [as soon as I saw it] with the first money I managed to save up [by] playing with The Yardbirds...I've had it ever since." Although according to Jerry Donahue in an interview with Tony Bacon, Clapton purchased his famous "Albert Hall" 335 when Jerry was working at Selmer's in 1968. This is uncorroborated, however there is little recorded use of Clapton playing the 335 until late in the Cream era. It is certainly a mystery. It is hard to think that Clapton would misremember a beloved guitar. However, for Donahue, meeting superstar/god (as he had been affectionately dubbed at the time) Eric Clapton on the day or so before the Albert Hall shows seem like something he would remember...we may never know. The dates and serial check out on Clapton's version, if like he said he bought it brand new, and the lack of further evidence or a second guitar seems to suggest the former, but that is simply speculation. The guitar in question sold for a whopping $847,500 and now belongs to Guitar Centre.

The association with Clapton and the incredible sounds he drew from the instrument inspired a whole new generation of players, many of whom tried to emulate through use of similar guitars and amplification. One such inspired player was a certain young virtuoso rock and fusion player from Austin, Texas, named Eric Johnson. Although he will probably be forever more associated with his 1954 Strat named "Virginia," Johnson has used 335's extensively throughout his career, frequently citing Clapton for inspiration on using 100-watt Marshalls and a cherry red ES-335. Many sources claim that his most famous recording, "Cliffs of Dover" from his 1990 album *Ah Via Musicom* was recorded on an ES-335, although there is not much information on that guitar, and whether it belonged to Johnson or whether he borrowed it. He has however owned a '64 335 since the mid-90's which he purchased from Gruhn Guitars, which has gone on to be one of his self-professed favourite instruments.

Another slightly unusual pioneer of the 335 was in fact none other than Ritchie Blackmore, of Deep Purple and later Rainbow fame. Ritchie's main guitar from 1962-1968 was a '61 335 and was used during his days in The Outlaws, his time backing Screaming Lord Sutch and all the way through to his early days in Purple. You can see this guitar in action in the videotapes of Deep Purple with the Royal Philharmonic Orchestra in 1968, and on the Child in Time video, from a set filmed for Granada television in 1970 (by which time he had switched to using mainly Stratocasters). When asked about this switch, Blackmore replied "It was difficult, because it's much easier to flow across the strings on a Gibson. Fenders have more tension, so you have to fight them a little bit. I had a hell of a time."

Aside from 335's, other ES guitars saw usage from the late 60's through to the 70s, such as Steve Howe and his 1964 ES-175D. Most famous for his role as guitarist for prog-rock legends Yes (along with forming supergroups Asia and GTR), Howe's 175D has been a constant staple, in about as different a context from the instrument's Rockabilly roots as it could possibly get. On how he came to find his lifelong companion, Howe said, "I yearned for that guitar. I wanted to start playing when I was 10 and I started when I was 12, and after a few years of playing Guyatone, Burns and things, just regular guitars, I had the courage to say to my mum and dad, "I want a really good guitar; I want one of these 175D things…" So, they said, "Okay, we'll help you," but I paid for it. Howe fell in love with this slightly unusual choice for a to-be rock star due to his love for Barney Kessel who famously used a Super 400CES, however, the 175D measured 16 inches wide, smaller than the 17-inch L-5CES or the 18-inch Super 400CES. It could well be said that this was the perfect, unconventional choice of guitar for Howe, who himself is an unconventional rock guitarist. Other notable users of the ES-175 include John Fogerty on the early Creedence Clearwater Revival records (until it was stolen out of his car), Pat Metheny, Izzy Stradlin of Guns 'n' Roses sometimes used a 175 in polar white finish, and at one time B.B. King.

The magic of these guitars is truly something wonderful. Even in the 21st century, these guitars are the weapon of choice for many musicians, whether they are well known or amateur. Sometimes affectionately referred to by those "in-the-know" as "Burst Killers," it is clear that they have something to them that sets them apart from the litany of guitars that populate the world—even the crazy rare, expensive, and most sought-after ones. Everybody from Dave Grohl of the Foo Fighters with his Pelham Blue Trini Lopez-inspired DG335 to Noel Gallagher, who made the 335 synonymous with Britpop in the 90s, to even the heaviest of music such as Magnus Pelander of Doom metal band Witchcraft, who uses an ES-137C, a short lived model introduced in Nashville during 2002, similar in appearance to the ES-175D, and built as a limited production run in the Memphis Custom Shop. Of course, there are other guitarists who carry the torch and continue to use these guitars for their more "traditional" blues role, with heavyweight names such as Gary Moore (until his untimely death in 2011), Joe Bonamassa, Kirk Fletcher, and Warren Haynes, who all have a good 335 amongst their arsenals. It is clear to see that whatever the future has in store for the guitar as an instrument, ES guitars will always play a heavy load-bearing role. It would be remiss not to mention at this point up and coming stars such as Marcus King, who is a testament to this, with Marcus playing his grandfather's vibrola-fitted ES-345 "Big Red," which has become one of the latest Gibson Custom Shop Signature ES models. Whether they are ultra-valuable and rare vintage examples or fresh off the production line at Gibson, or even one of the thousands of copy models "inspired by" Gibson's ES designs, their spread reaches all corners of the Eart—and it is highly unusual to find any guitarist who has been touched to any extent by "The Bug" not to have at least something ES-esque in their collection. These guitars are genuinely an all-round understated staple of music as a whole, and certainly will continue to be for many years to come.

feature written by Jonas Stanley

B.B. KING (1925 - 2015)

For more than half a century, Riley B. King—better known as B.B. King—has defined the blues for a worldwide audience. He was born September 16, 1925, on a plantation in Itta Bena, Mississippi, near Indianola. In his youth, he played on street corners for dimes, and would sometimes play in as many as four towns a night. In 1947, he hitchhiked to Memphis, Tennessee to pursue his music career. Memphis was where every important musician of the South gravitated, and which supported a large musical community where every style of African American music could be found. B.B. stayed with his cousin Bukka White, one of the most celebrated blues performers of his time, who schooled B.B. further in the art of the blues. B.B.'s first big break came in 1948 when he performed on Sonny Boy Williamson's radio program on KWEM out of West Memphis. This led to steady engagements at the Sixteenth Avenue Grill in West Memphis, and later to a ten-minute spot on black-staffed and managed Memphis radio station WDIA. "King's Spot" became so popular, it was expanded and became the "Sepia Swing Club." Soon, B.B. needed a catchy radio name. What started out as Beale Street Blues Boy was shortened to Blues Boy King, and eventually B.B. King. In the mid-1950s, while B.B. was performing at a dance in Twist, Arkansas, a few fans became unruly. Two men got into a fight and knocked over a kerosene stove, setting fire to the hall. B.B. raced outdoors to safety with everyone else, then realized that he left his beloved $30 acoustic guitar inside, so he rushed back inside the burning building to retrieve it, narrowly escaping death. When he later found out that the fight had been over a woman named Lucille, he decided to give the name to his guitar to remind him never to do a crazy thing like fight over a woman. Ever since, each one of B.B.'s trademark Gibson guitars has been called Lucille. Soon after his number one hit, "Three O'Clock Blues," B.B. began touring nationally. Over the years, B.B. has developed one of the world's most identifiable guitar styles. He borrowed from Blind Lemon Jefferson, T-Bone Walker and others, integrating his precise and complex vocal-like string bends and his left hand vibrato, both of which have become indispensable components of rock guitarist's vocabulary. His economy, his every-note-counts phrasing, has been a model for thousands of players, from Eric Clapton and George Harrison to Jeff Beck. B.B. has mixed traditional blues, jazz, swing, mainstream pop and jump into a unique sound. In B.B.'s words, "When I sing, I play in my mind; the minute I stop singing orally, I start to sing by playing Lucille." B.B. was inducted into the Blues Foundation Hall of Fame in 1984 and into the Rock and Roll Hall of Fame in 1987. B.B. continued to tour extensively, averaging over 250 concerts per year around the world. Classics such as "Payin' The Cost To Be The Boss," "The Thrill Is Gone," "How Blue Can You Get," "Everyday I Have The Blues," and "Why I Sing The Blues" are concert (and fan) staples. B.B.'s most popular crossover hit, 1970s "The Thrill Is Gone" went to numbmer 15 on the Hot 100 chart.
B.B. passed away in his sleep on May 14th, 2015.   *Extracted from www.bbking.com*

JEFF BECK (1944 - 2023)

As we compiled ES Believers, we heard of the sudden untimely passing of Jeff Beck and offer condolences to his wife Sandra, and the family. Tributes have poured in from the guitar world who recognised Jeff as a true master of the guitar, and it is unlikely anyone will ever take his place. No matter which brand of guitar passed through his hands, he produced that unmistakable tone. In 2012, he paid tribute to Les Paul at the Iridium Club in New York, and the ES-175 was the guitar he used on "Baby Let's Play House," playing some great Scotty Moore licks.

Thank you, Jeff for the wonderful music you created...
David and Vic

1958 ES-335 Cherry Red
A28800

According to the book, Gibson Electrics, The Classic Years by A.R. Duchossoir (Hal Leonard, 1994) Gibson records show that one ES 335 T was completed on December 15, 1958, and was finished in cherry red more than a year before the color was officially offered as an option. That guitar was given serial number A 28800. This particular 335 was equipped with factory stereo wiring. The guitar was found in Northern California and eventually sold to St. Louis dealer Dave Hinson. Dave reports the guitar was used by the original owner as collateral for a loan that was never re-paid. Dave also said the guitar was in near-mint condition with all of the original paperwork and tags. This particular 335 has pearl dot inlays where the stop tailpiece would go and is equipped with a Bigsby tailpiece. Also included in the deal was a Gibson GA-83 Stereo-Vib amp, serial number 118180, with owner's manual and schematic. At last report, this gem was resting in England.

Thanks to Dave Hinson for this feature

1959 Super 400 CES

Originally introduced in 1934, the Super 400 was Gibson's most expensive guitar. It was called the Super 400 because it cost $400.00. The cost was more than most working people made in two months at their jobs. During the 1950s, this guitar became the Super 400 CES with the addition of P-90 pickups and a slightly thicker top to reduce feedback. In 1957, this model was equipped with the new humbucking pickups.

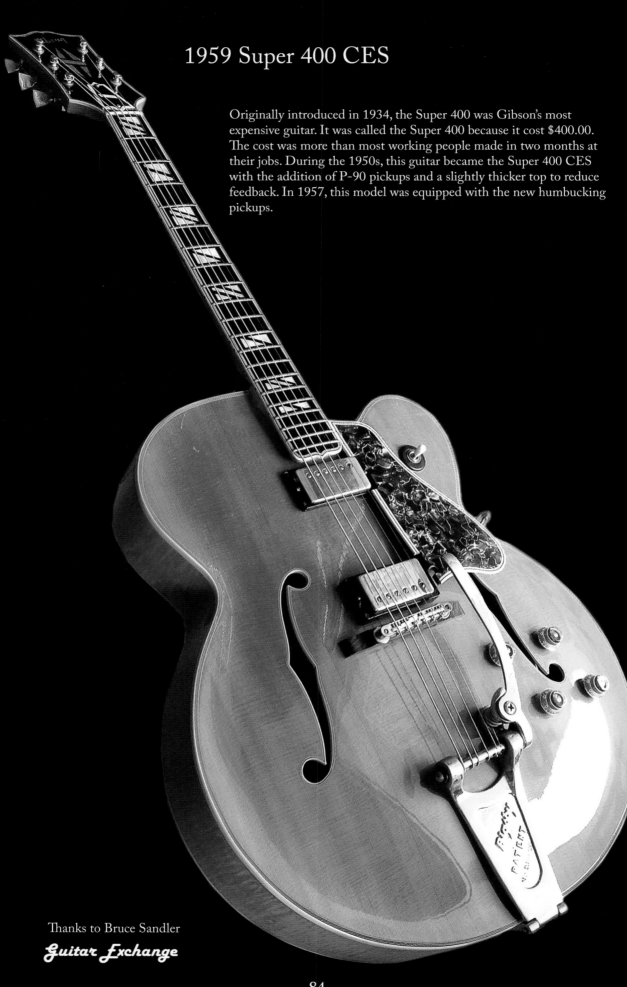

Thanks to Bruce Sandler

Guitar Exchange

Super 400 CES

The crowning touch ... developed through years of research, the Super 400 CES has been enthusiastically acclaimed by outstanding musicians everywhere as the finest electric Spanish guitar. Superior materials and superb Gibson craftsmanship have been combined to provide this luxurious instrument with its clear, clean-cut powerful tone and dependable performance.

Hand-graduated, carved top of finest spruce • carved back of highly figured curly maple • curly maple rims with alternate black and white ivoroid binding • modern cutaway design • small, comfortable feeling three-piece curly maple neck with Gibson Adjustable Truss Rod • multiple-bound ebony fingerboard with distinctive pearl inlays • exclusive peghead design with pearl inlays • Tune-O-Matic bridge permits adjustment of string action and individual string lengths for perfect intonation • twin, powerful pickups placed for contrasting treble and bass response • individually adjustable polepieces • separate tone and volume controls which can be preset • toggle switch to activate either or both pickups • gold-plated metal parts • exclusive Super 400 Varitone tailpiece • hand-bound pickguard deluxe individual machine heads.

SPECIFICATIONS
18" wide, 21¾" long, 3⅜" deep, 25½" scale, 20 frets

Super 400 CESN—Natural Finish	$700.00
Super 400 CES—Golden Sunburst Finish	675.00
No. 400 Case—Faultless, plush lined	60.00
No. ZC-4 Zipper Case Cover	30.00

A FAVORITE OF THE LEADING GUITARISTS

1959 ES-345 TDS
A31733

Elvin Bishop and "Red Dog"

Elvin Bishop moved to Chicago in 1960. On his first day in the Windy City, he met Paul Butterfield. Elvin joined The Paul Butterfield Blues Band and recorded four albums with them. The first two albums featured Mike Bloomfield. In Elvin's words, he didn't play to much on the first two albums because Bloomfield was such an accomplished player and getting a lot of recognition. Bloomfield left the band and Elvin was the main guitarist for the last two albums which were "The Resurrection of Pig Boy Crabshaw" and "In My Own Dream." While in Chicago, Bishop met blues guitarist Louis Myers at a show. Elvin persuaded Myers to trade him his Cherry Gibson ES 345 for his Fender Telecaster. Myers obliged and that guitar has remained with Elvin since the early 1960s and still gets played to this day. I would imagine more in the studio these days than live performances. The ES-345 is either a 1959 or 1960. The guitar got named in later years by an Allman Brothers roadie. He called it "Red Dog."

Elvin's choice of amps was an Ampeg flip top and Fender Twin Reverbs. In 1968, Elvin went solo and moved to San Francisco. This was around the summer of love era as he called it. He played on the LP "The Live Adventures of Mike Bloomfield and Al Kooper." Bloomfield got sick, and Elvin stepped in and handled the lead guitar role. The Elvin Bishop Band signed with Fillmore Records which was owned by Bill Graham, who formed the Fillmore music venues. In March of 1971, The Elvin Bishop Band and The Allman Brothers Band co-billed a series of concerts at the Fillmore East.

Elvin was inducted into the Rock & Roll Hall of Fame in 2015 as an original member of The Paul Butterfield Blues Band. However, he was more excited about being inducted to The Blues Hall of Fame in Memphis. Some noteworthy tunes of TEBB are Travelin' Shoes (some really nice harmony leads in this song), Sure Feels Good, and Struttin' My Stuff, but Elvin will be most remembered for his big hit "Fooled Around And Fell In Love," featuring Mickey Thomas.

Thanks to Elvin for providing the information for this feature

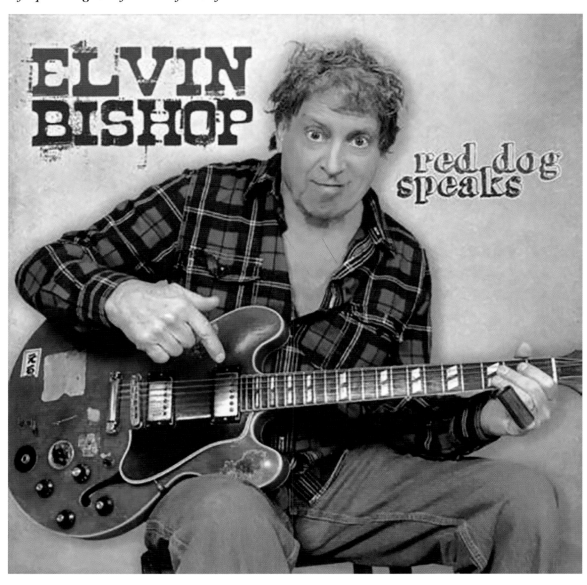

89

1959 ES-335 Dot

Formerly owned by Peter Green, then Victor Brox (UK Blues keyboardist), then John Morshead (UK guitarist), and then Jackie Lomax who bought it in 1969 and owned it until his death in 2013.

Thanks to Charlie Gelber and John Ladas for this feature

1959 Blond ES-335
Dot Neck
A 30864

This example features a big profile neck consistent with most early to mid '59 ES models. The orange oval label inside the bass "F" hole shows the guitar's serial number. Impressed serial numbers started in 1961 with the serial numbers placed on the back of the headstock and inside the "F" hole.

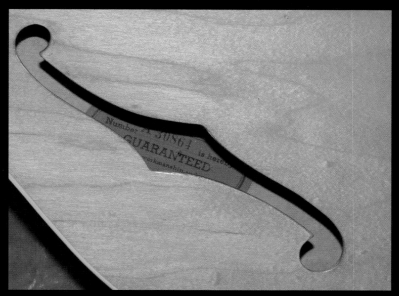

1959 ES-335
A 30521

Thanks to Ben Brion,
Le Guitarium, Paris, France.

Photo credit: Rodolphe Bricard.

94

1959 ES-345
A 32141

Submitted by Chris Soucy
Photo credit: Allison Tyler

1957 ES-225 TN
FON U2244 35

1960 ES330-TN
FON R3563 6

The Bob Wootton Collection

1959 ES-335TD
A 30563

1961 ES-330TC
40479

Rusty Anderson

1959 ES-335
Blond Dot Neck

Photo credit: Bill Bernstein

At 14, I was inspired to get a Gibson 335 after seeing my friend, Richard Ballou, play in a band called "Kick." He had a 60s cherry red one and was a local guitar hero. He eventually became a good friend. Two years later, my band "Eulogy" opened up for Van Halen at the Golden West Ballroom. Eddie was also playing a red 335 and I was impressed.

Later on, my friend Nick Panicci who bought, sold and collected guitars, amps, clothes, etc., had a nice '65 cherry red 335. I got really excited when I played it because it had amazing action and a banjo-ish, magical midrange tone. Being semi-hollow, it had a slightly ethnic tonal quality that I was smitten by. It's a bit hard to put into words. Anyway, I begged and pleaded with him to sell it to me and he finally agreed. I still have the guitar and love it. Sonically and feel-wise, 335's really vary from year to year, ranging from about 7 1/2 pounds on up to about 9 pounds: quite heavy.

Not long after I started touring with Paul McCartney, I sought out a vintage blonde 335, mostly because that finish wasn't so popular at the time. I finally found a nice one and bought it from Drew Berlin. That became my main axe for quite a while. It's relatively lightweight, very responsive, great action, nice neck shape.

A few years later, Pat Foley from Gibson approached me about designing a signature model. I was very happy when they agreed to make specific changes that brought the signature guitars much closer to my original '59 they were based on. And by the way, a shout-out to Mike Voltz, Jim Lillard, and the fantastic Gibson team is in order. After the third prototype, we were ready to release it. I was ecstatic to have gotten fantastic feedback on the guitar model…no pun intended.

Rusty

Photo credit: Tamarind Free Jones

1959 ES-355
A 30376

This sunburst ES-355 is the one and only one made in 1959 in this finish

1962 ES-355 TD-N
with ebony block

1959 ES-335
A 30585

1959 ES-335
A-30188

Photo credit: Lou Gatanas

1959 ES-345 Blond
A 31898

The blond ES-345 is quite a rare guitar. Only 32 were made in 1959, and 18 in 1960 bringing a total of only 50 produced. These models have a rosewood fingerboard like the 335, but have the stereo varitone switch added for additional tones out of the PAFs.

Also, this model sports parallelogram neck inlays, kluson gold tuners and gold hardware. Notice the photo of the original owner, along with the original stereo guitar cable and strap.

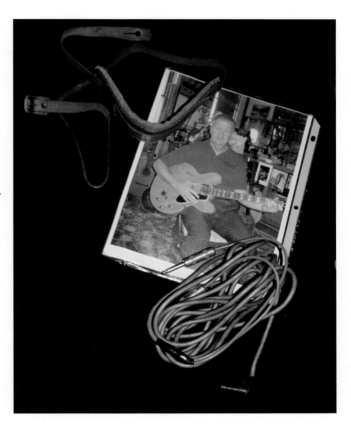

1959 ES-345
A 30605
a factory black custom order

1959 ES-345 Cherry
A 31536

Thanks to Trey Rabinek for this feature

1964 ES-335 Cherry
168019

I flew to Ohio to buy this guitar in 2022. The original owner bought this in high school in 1964 at Dusi Music in Youngstown, Ohio.

The original owner, Alan, with his '64 ES-335

1959 ES-335 Sunburst
A 31585

Previous page
I flew to New York to buy this guitar in 2017. In 1968, a mechanic outside of Boston took this guitar in trade from a customer who could not afford to pay in cash. He did not play guitar, so it remained in his closet for the next 50 years. I met up with the family in 2017 and was able to buy the guitar, which is 100% original.

Elliot Easton - The Cars

I was 10 years old in 1964 and like all kids first discovering the world of electric guitars I fixated on Gretsch and Rickenbacker. Soon after, I wanted to know more, especially about the gleaming cherry-red hollow bodies that said Gibson on the headstock. There was just something magical about them...they looked like they came out of a dream to me. Soon, I was seeing all kinds of artists playing them on all the 60's music shows like "Shindig!" and "Hullaballoo," and it wasn't long before I went to Sam Ash in Huntington, Long Island. I just can't overstate how amazing it was back then to actually see these guitars in person—they just looked, well, famous! I walked out of the store with the green '66 Gibson catalog, the one with the trees on the cover. I took that thing to school and hid it behind my textbooks and did my real studying. I could have told you the code number for the zipper case covers! BTW, I still have the catalog. What else to say about the ES Series? From blues rockers like Eric Clapton, Alvin Lee, Elvin Bishop and even early Richie Blackmore to guys like Larry Carlton and Robben Ford, who play blues, jazz, funk and all points in between, to the Nashville A-Team masters like Grady Martin and Hank Garland, to the great bluesmen like B.B. King and Freddie King, one fact becomes crystal clear:

YOU CAN PLAY ANY KIND OF MUSIC ON A GIBSON ES MODEL!

Best,
EE

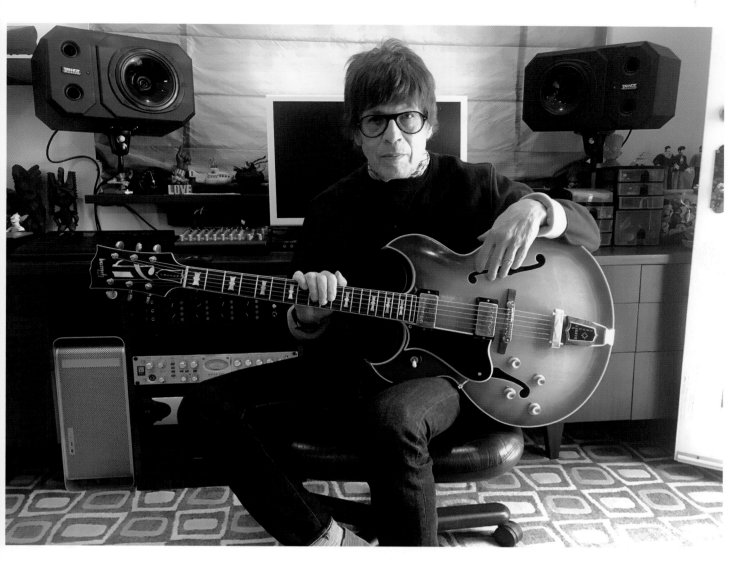

1965 Trini Lopez   1964/5 ES-335   1962 Barney Kessel

1959 Blond ES-355
A 31528

1959 Blond ES 355 A 31528...super rare, this blond 355 was a special order guitar (see ledger). The natural finish on this guitar is the first time Gibson used it on a 355. It is the only natural finished 355 produced in 1959. It's one of one. Note the pickguard is not tortoise shell, it's a black long guard as used on a 335 or 345 from this era. Quite a rare specimen !!

JOE BROWN, MBE

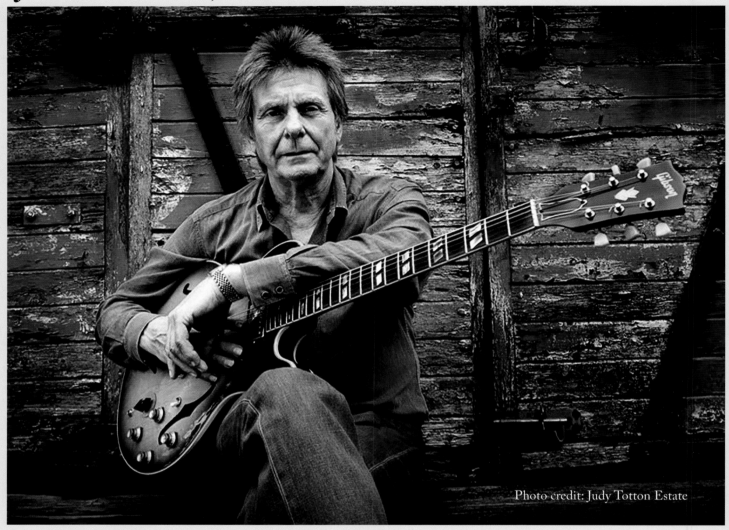

Photo credit: Judy Totton Estate

"I've always used Gibsons ever since I could afford one. My first was an electric 335 Dot neck, which I used on all my sessions including those for other artists and of course on stage myself. For an acoustic, I now use a small Gibson B25 with an early Takamine pickup fitted by a luthier in Nashville—Great sound!"

JOE BROWN, MBE

Joe with a stellar line up of stars from the 1960s

Left to right:

Bill Fury, Jess Condrad, Gene Vincent, Joe Brown, Eddic Cochrane, Adam Faith and Marty Wilde.

Joe Brown is a well-loved and respected artist from London with a string of hits in the 1960s. He is more known for his vocal talents but is a great guitarist playing Gibson guitars. His performance at the George Harrison tribute Concert for George 2002 at the Royal Albert Hall, where he closed the show, is one of the most poignant moments in rock history.

We thank Joe and his manager John Taylor for this feature

TOM BUKOVAC

I have been a major proponent of the pre-mid 1965 Gibson ES-335 for many
years. I always considered it to be the most perfect electric guitar design of
all time. A solid chunk of rock and roll with two "feedback wings" that
give you perfectly controllable feedback when you turn just the right way to
the amp. Amazing guitars.

Tom

1959 ES-335
A30906

Very few models were produced in a cherry finish in 1959 and 1960.
However, cherry became a standard color in 1961.

1959 ES-335
A32174

1959 ES-330 TD

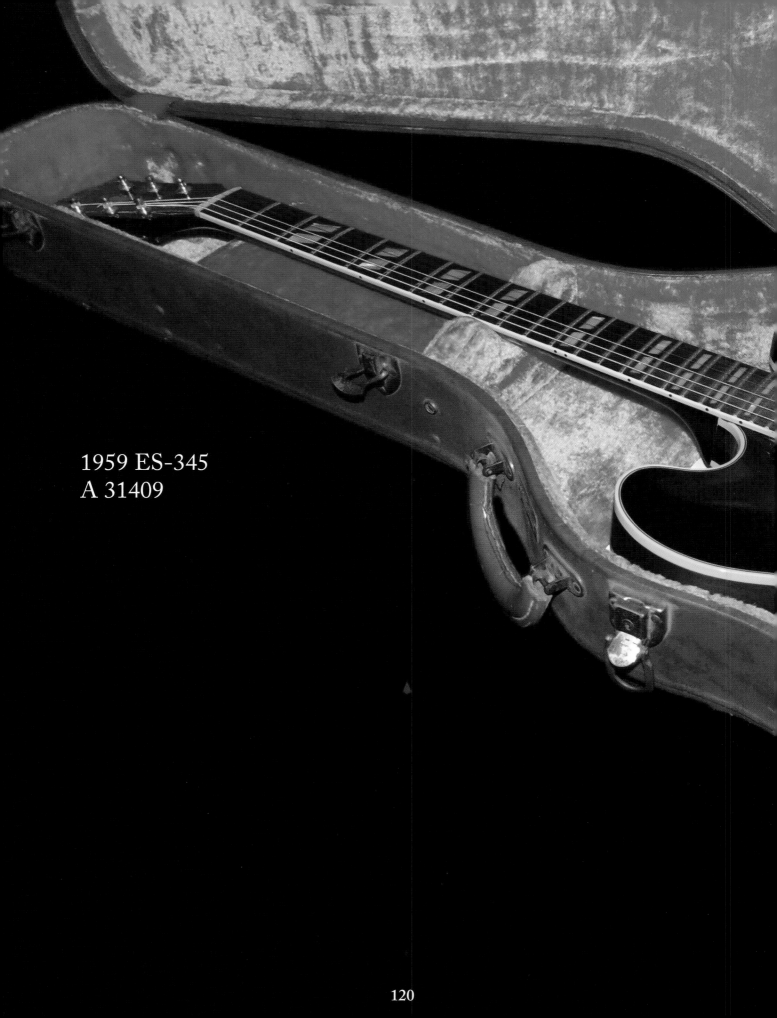

1959 ES-345
A 31409

FORD THURSTON

Growing up as a kid in Pittsburgh, my heroes were Jeff Beck, Van Halen, Hendrix and all the Blues kings. Back in those days, I used to ride my bicycle out to Route 19 to this cool little shop called Guitar Gallery. There I would be always eyeing up these little pointy headstock guitars, but the guys that worked there would tell me that what I needed was a vintage Gibson. So, one day I finally caved in and bought one, and I've never looked back. For years I exclusively played Gibson Les Pauls and SGs. Then on a cold winter's day, I was on tour in Michigan, and I finally found that vintage 1960 Gibson ES 335. And that was it! It's the greatest guitar ever made. It's warm, it's got a soft top end, and perfect mids and lows. It's an awesome guitar when you're hanging at the house on the couch—it's the perfect couch guitar—plus mine has a Bigsby tremolo arm, which helps me express myself like a vocalist. The 335 fits your body like a glove and once you strap it on, you're an acolyte for life. For me, it's the be all, end all, of all guitars. If I had to pick one desert island guitar, it'd be my 1960 Gibson 335 forever. All my guitar heroes as a kid, Jeff, Jimi, Eddie, the 335 can handle all of it. So, thank you, Vic DaPra, for showing me the light. You can find me in Nashville, playing, producing or touring out on the road with different artists.

1959   1960

Photo credit: Jon Roncolato

1959 ES-330 T

1959 ES-355 Mono
A29658

WARREN HAYNES

My attraction to ES style guitars started when I was a kid seeing my guitar heroes playing them. I currently own a 1961 Cherry ES-335. These guitars have a uniqueness to them like no others. They have an acoustic nature to their sound. The Gibson Custom Shop did a great job on my signature '61 ES-335. It has the same feel and looks as my original one. With Government Mule I use my signature Les Paul, other Les Paul Reissues, Firebirds and my signature 335 along with a Custom Shop blond 335. As far as 335s being Burst killers, my opinion is they are two different guitars. One can do what the other can't. I don't travel with my Burst and '61 Dot anymore however I do use them in the studio. As far as amps, I use Homestead amps and my old modified Soldano.

Warren

Photo credit: Charlie Daughtry

129

1959 ES-330 TD-N

Cajun Blues man Tony Joe White played a blond
ES 330-TD on "Polk Salad Annie" Gator's Gotch'
Your Granny, Chomp, Chomp, Chomp.

1959 ES-345
A31146

Submitted by: Nino Fazio, Messina Italy

1959 ES-335
A 30518
1958 FON

1959 Gibson ES-335TD #A30519

Original Factory
Serial Number Log
showing when this
guitar was shipped.

ES-335.T	A·30516		JUNE 22 1959
ES-335.T	A·30517		
ES-335.T	A·30518		
ES-335.T	A·30519		
ES-335.T	A·30520		

Photo credit: Bill Fajen

133

Howard Leese

When I was 15, my band The ZOO got discovered and got a record deal. Convinced that I may have a future in music, my Mom went down with me to ACE Music in Santa Monica to get me a good guitar. I was thinking Firebird, but when I played a new for 1966 Watermelon ES-335, I knew that was the one for me. There is something about a thin line semi-hollow body that just feels right. You get a bit of the body sound that gives your tone a depth and richness that is unique.
I still have this guitar and I played it on many Heart recordings.

Howard Leese
Malibu, 2023

1959 Blond ES 330T

Howard and Joe Bonamassa are checking out a 1959 Blond ES 345

I purchased this ES 335 new in 1966

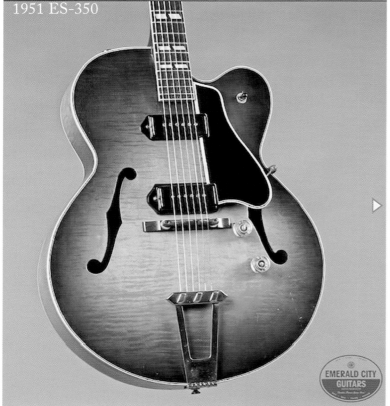
1951 ES-350

EMERALD CITY GUITARS

1960 ES-345

134

Here I am today with my '66 ES 335

Thank Howard for this great feature
Vic and David

1959 ES-335 T
A30251, FON T7281 25

KEITH RICHARDS

Keith is shown here with a scarce, hard to find original 1959 black ES 355. He is by far the coolest cat that plays a thinline ES model. Keep on rockin' Keef.

This original white finish 1964 ES-345 is nicknamed "Dwight"

1959 Blond ES –335
A 31331

Thanks to Zac Arch

1959 ES-345   G.E.Smith
A31158

This original double pickguard factory mono 1959 ES-345 was owned and played by G.E. Smith. He used this particular guitar on many Hall & Oates recordings (Sara Smile, Rich Girl, Man Eater, Private Eyes and many more) as well as Mick Jagger's solo record, Diana Ross, plus Bob Dylan's many recordings and tours. G.E. used this guitar on the television show *Saturday Night Live* Christmas Eve show for 10 years. This is an extremely rare piece of American history and guitar television history. There is a handwritten letter of authenticity from G.E. Smith with lots of film footage and pictures of this guitar with many famous people.

Photo credit: Martyn Turner

Thanks to RJ for this feature

1957 ES-225 TD

1959 ES-345
(A31271-FON S9631 27)

Photo credit: James Michael Lubbard

Thanks to JT Guitars

THOMAS TULL
of *The Ghosthounds*

The Gibson semi-hollow body ES-335s have a sound that's very distinct and all their own. Rock and roll was invented on it, from Chuck Berry to the sweet sounds of B.B. King. My main guitar is a Gibson Les Paul but when you need that rock and roll swagger, there's nothing like it.

Thomas

1959 ES 335
A 30061

A pair of 1959 ES-330 TDs

1960 ES-330 TD

1960 ES-330 TDC
FON R3310 19

1960 ES-345
R-6544-6 Custom order

Drew Berlin is shown here with an extremely rare 1960 white ES-345 which has been aptly nicknamed "The White Unicorn."

Thanks to Matt Swnason and Drew Berlin

Thanks to Tadahiko Okazaki

1960 ES-330 N
R 3356 25

Owned by Brent Coleman, photographed by Derek Bruneau

1960 ES-335
A 35205

155

1960 Mono ES-355
A 32828

Photo credit: Charlie Gelber
OK Guitars

Dave Edmunds
1960 ES-335 TDN

One of the great exponents of the ES-335, Dave Edmunds had hits such as "I hear you Knocking" and instrumental, "Sabre Dance." He used this iconic 335 for most of his career and spent almost 20 years recording and producing in Rockfield Studios near his home in Monmouth, Wales.

"Taken during a visit to my store, Guitars R Us back in early 2001. Dave dropped by to show me his well-played and beloved 1960 ES-335 TDN."
Photo and quote, Albert Molinaro

Photo credit: Jay Rosen

1960 ES-355 mono
A 34309

A vibrant cherry red, no Varitone, with twin PAFs and
factory Bigsby. The Gibson Crestline amp fans will also
get a buzz out of the 1964 GA19 RVT Falcon amplifier
acting as a guitar stand.

Owned by Brent Coleman, photographed by Derek Bruneau

1960 ES-5 Switchmaster
A32976

Thanks to Simon Gauf
GuitarPoint

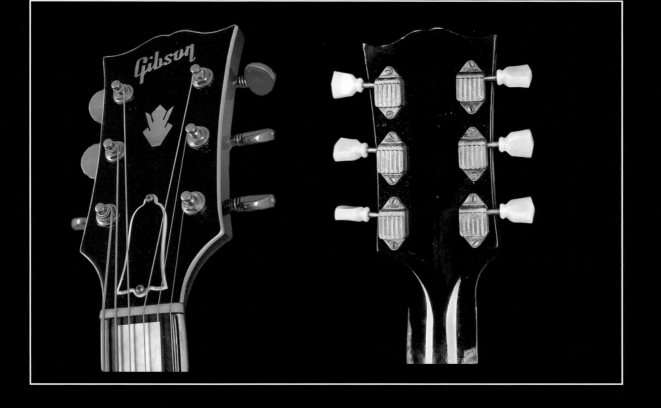

Photo credit: Mike Slubowski

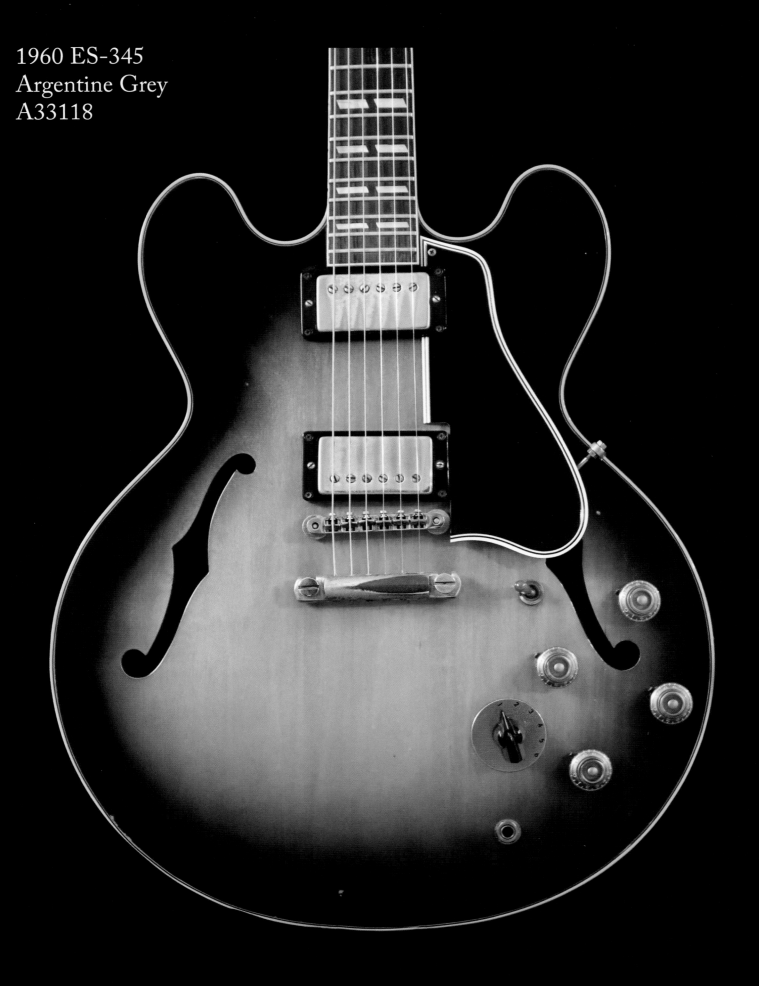

1960 ES-345
Argentine Grey
A33118

1960 ES-355 TDSV
A34313

From The Thomas Tull Collection

1960 ES-345
A33143

Thanks to Steve Gornall
Photo credit: Albert Molinaro

1961 ES-335
A 35705

An early 1961, this 335 still sports a long pickguard
and an autograph on the face from B.B. King.

We want to thank Barney Roach for this submission.
Photography by Rick Gould

KIRK FLETCHER

I use and have used a Gibson ES 335 since the beginning of my career because so many of my influences used that particular model. It's a guitar that really marries my major influences. They are blues artists like B.B. King, Freddie King, Shuggie Otis plus funky players like Ray Parker Junior and the great David Williams at one time. Then you have my other major influences like Larry Carlton, Robben Ford, Chris Cain and a host of others.

For me, it's the singing quality and versatility that just speaks to me. It's just one of the best Blues guitars ever made in my opinion. The sound of the 335 will be in my mind for the rest of my days.

Thanks to Drew Berlin's Vintage Guitars for this feature

1960 ES-335
A 34479

Originally a Bigsby equipped 335, this one was
converted to a stop tailpiece.

Photo credit: Allison Tyler
photo submission : Chris Soucy

1960 ES-355 TD
A 33369

Mono/stop tail and a special wiring that gets an
out-of-phase sound in the middle position

Photo credit: Giovana Pili
Thanks to Jacques Menache Masri

1960 ES-355 TDC
A-32831

Submitted by: Nino Fazio, Messina Italy

1960 ES-345
A-32606

Thanks to Matt for this feature

1960 ES-335 TD-N
A 33408

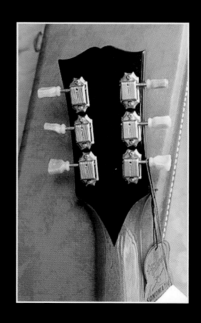

1960 ES-345
A 33896

One of the two ES's Alan has owned

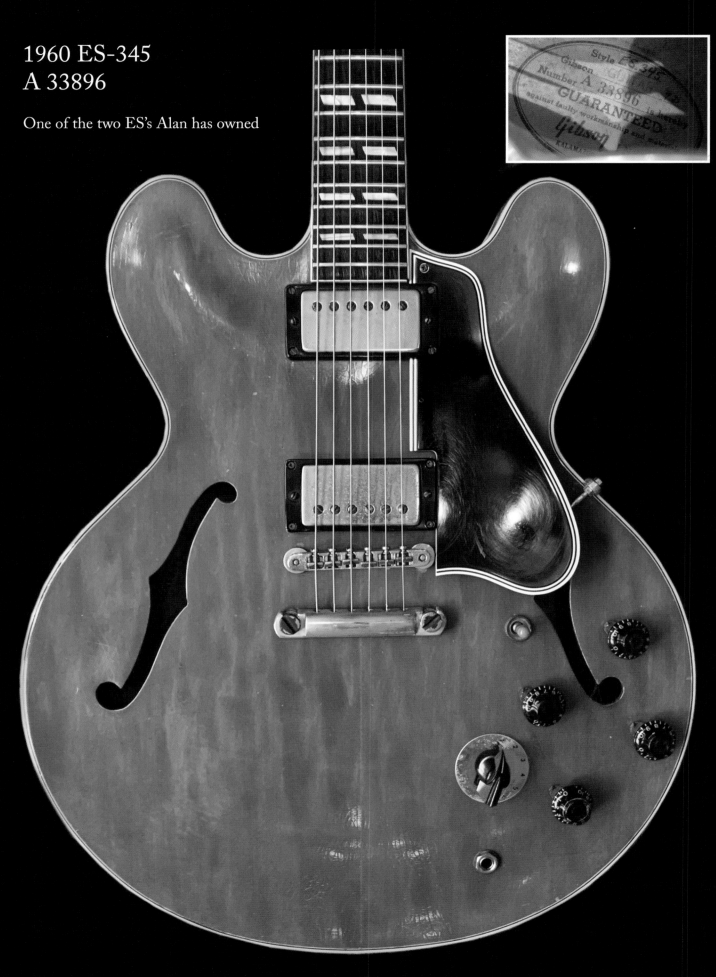

ALAN DARBY r.i.p.

Alan Darby (d. 2023) was a successful Scottish guitarist, singer and songwriter.

He was sideman for Van Morrison, Robert Palmer, Eric Clapton (playing alongside him at his Crossroads 2019 fundraiser festival in Dallas), John Martyn, Bonnie Tyler and many others.

He co-wrote with Bonnie Raitt, and Queen's Brian May chose him as one of the two principal guitarists for the original London *We Will Rock You* show for its entire 10-year run. Although best remembered for his pioneering use of Firebirds, he used this versatile guitar on many sessions and library tracks as well as his own ultimate album, Rolling Man.

Bob Wootton, Alan's tech 2016–23

Thanks to Rick Zsigmond, Bob Wootton amd new owner Dekel Bor

DEKEL BOR

"Dekel Bor's evocative live guitar playing...a fresh taste in music"

(John Rockwell, New York Times)

Dekel Bor has performed with the Israel philharmonic orchestra, recorded with Alicia Keys, collaborated with John Scofield, and was mentored by Reggie Workman & Jim Hall. He was shortlisted for four Grammy awards, including "Jazz Album of the Year."

Style *ES 335*
Gibson GUITAR TD
Number A 33574 is hereby
GUARANTEED
against faulty workmanship and materials.

Photo credit: Masha Vesset

1960 ES-335 Dot Neck
A 33574
FON R 455 33

1960 ES-335 Dot Neck
A 33605

This 335 is a mid-year production model with a medium/slim profile neck and features '59 appointments such as a long pickguard, bonnet knobs and single ring kluson tuners.

1960 ES-335

This once-owned Joe Bonamassa 335 was played on the Beth Hart records and on tours.

Photo credit: Dag Lutyen

1960 ES-355 TDSV
A34225

Thanks to Simon Gauf
GuitarPoint

184

1960 ES-355 TD
A 34333

Style ES-355 TD
Gibson
Number A 34333 is hereby
GUARANTEED
against faulty workmanship and materials
Gibson INC
KALAMAZOO

Thanks toRick Zsigmond
NewKings Road Guitars

Photo credit: Mo Panella

1960 BLOND EB 2-N
A 33058

Note the banjo style tuners used on this bass. Gibson used these on this model in 1959 and 1960

Submitted by Chris Soucy
Photo credit: Allison Tyler

Incredible photos of such a
fine and rare mono ES-355

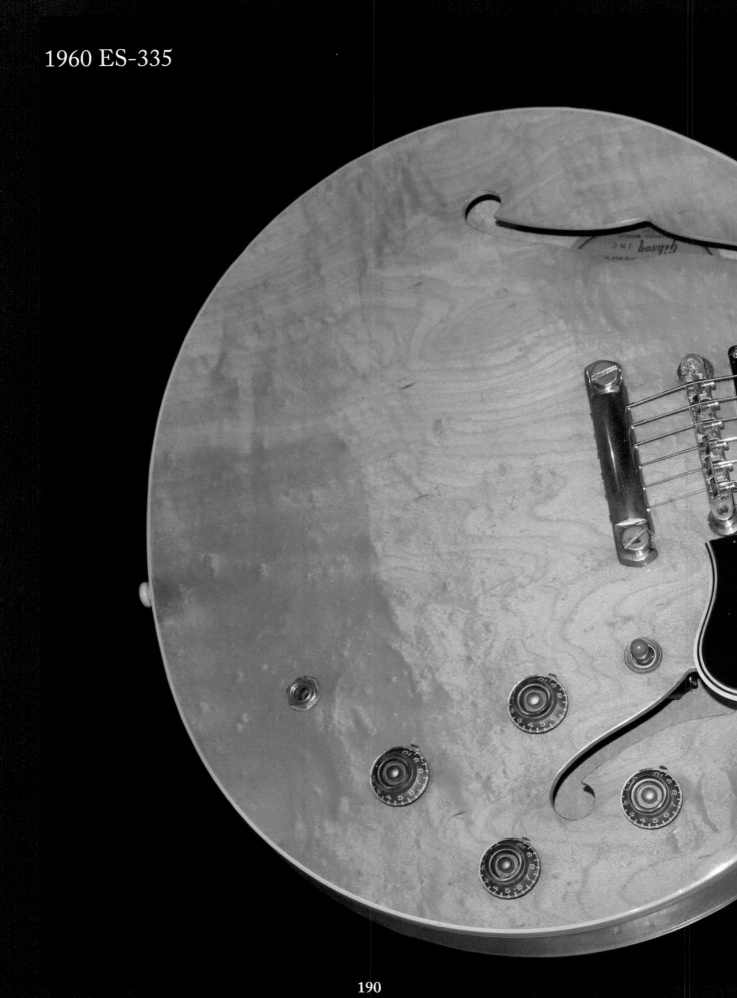

A family-owned guitar, which came with a Tweed Gibson Vanguard Amp

Gary's Classic Guitars/Ben Isaacs

1960 ES-355
A 33245

1960 ES-330

Thanks to Bernie Marsden

1960 Blonde ES-345
A 33831

194

1960 ES-335 TD-N
A 33435 "Barney"

This Blond 335 was found by my friend Roger Hoard. The original owner's family had it stored in a barn, hence the name "Barney" was given to it. A mid-year 1960 with a slim neck. It does not have the ultra-slim neck as a late 1960. This dot has the features of a '59 with its long pickguard and bonnet knobs and single ring tuners, also a factory stinger at the bottom of the neck.

1961 ES-345 TD
17154 LH

Photo credit: Rumble Seat Music   Thanks to David Proler

1961 mono ES-355

Thanks to Binky Philips for this trio of ES's.

200

1959 Blond ES-225 T

1966 ES-345

This 1966 ES-345 sports the ultra rare Pelham Blue finish

1961 Blond Byrdland

Photography by Jon Roncolato,
Carter Vintage Guitars

TED NUGENT

Ted Nugent is an American rocker who played with The Amboy Dukes, Damn Yankees, and his own band. He had such notable hits as "Journey to the Center of Your Mind," "Cat Scratch Fever," and "Stranglehold." He was noted for using a Gibson Byrdland to great effect, controlling the feedback the guitar would produce to fit his style, which was high-energy rock and roll.

1962 ES-345 Cherry Dot
44270

One of the last of the '62
Dot Necks with 2 PAFs

Photo credit: Bill Fajen

204

1962 Cherry ES-330 – 55043

Photo credit: Dave Keeling

1961 Byrdland TD
39785

1962 E-350 TN
80944

JUSTIN HAYWARD
of The Moody Blues

"I saw Joe Brown at McIlroys in Swindon and I fell in love with that guitar. I even like the sometimes clanky sound they can have, but nothing speaks or sings quite like a 335. They have personality.

I bought my first 335 new in 1963, but I had to sell it not long before I joined the Moodies because I was broke. In 1968, at Selmers in Charing Cross Road, I found the '63 ES 335 that I've had ever since. Through an amp or a processor, or even unplugged, my 335 always delivers.

It's my dearest friend."

Justin Hayward

Thanks to Justin Hayward and James Ianocha for this feature.

1961 ES-330 T

Photo credit: Raul Barrios

1963 ES-330 T

1962 ES-355 (Tuxedo)
25409

White ES guitars from the golden era are
extremely rare and beautiful

Photography: Rick Gould - Guitar property of Bonaseum

213

1962 ES-345
85170

1960 ES-335
A33432

1964 ES-345
68405

ES-335
26547

Yes, even Ritchie Blackmore, who is commonly associated with the Fender Stratocaster, once played a dot-neck Gibson ES-335. Ritchie's association with this guitar was due to his fascination with Tom Harvey of the band "Nero and the Gladiators." So, in 1962 he purchased a cherry red dot neck ES-335 serial number 26547. Ritchie played this guitar throughout the 1960s and very early 1970s. Most, if not all, of the guitar tracks on Deep Purple's groundbreaking 1970 album *In Rock* were played on the 335. The band's famous appearance in 1969 at Royal Albert Hall "Concerto for Group and Orchestra" was all done using the Cherry Dot. He switched to a Stratocaster in the early 1970s because he liked the metallic sound the guitar produced.

RITCHIE BLACKMORE

1963 ES-125T
272149

1964 ES-125 TDC
158230

Photo credit: Albert Molinaro

1960 ES-335 TD
A-35538

This particular guitar has the later 1960 slim tapered neck

1965 ES-335TDC
281644

Big neck, stop tailpiece and cherry finish makes this a very sought-after guitar.

This Marshall amp is a 1967 JTM Tremolo model aka the "Bluesbreaker"

BERNIE MARSDEN

WHITESNAKE

1964 ES-345
181758

My first memories of the ES guitars are on black and white TV. 1960s bands were numerous on television and most of the guitar players used an ES-345 or 335, with an occasional appearance of a 330. My theory is that the bands spent their advance on the most expensive gear, which explains why the ES 345 was very popular! Post-Cream, a plethora of guitar players discovered the brilliance of an original ES-335; it was so versatile, looked cool and sounded great. I've been fortunate to own a few of these instruments in my time and found an original ES-335 to be one of the most useful guitars in my collection, if you exclude my ES-T-150 Tenor guitar!

Enjoy the gems in the book.

Bernie
April 2023

1963 ES-345
103438

Thanks to Simon Gauf
GuitarPoint

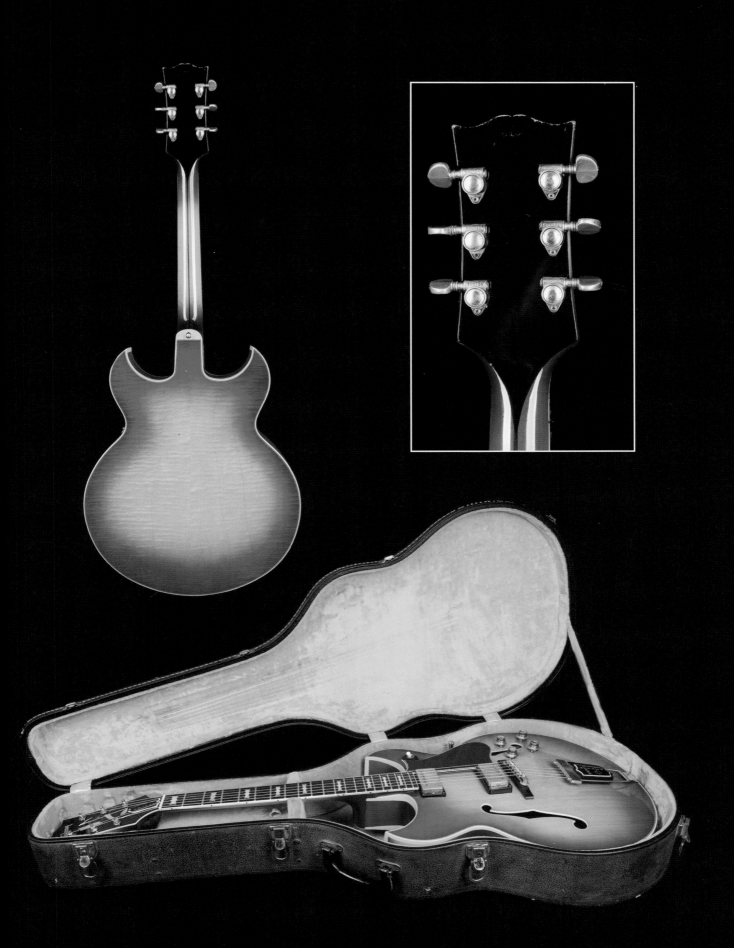

Submitted by: Nino Fazio, Messina Italy

BARRIE CADOGAN

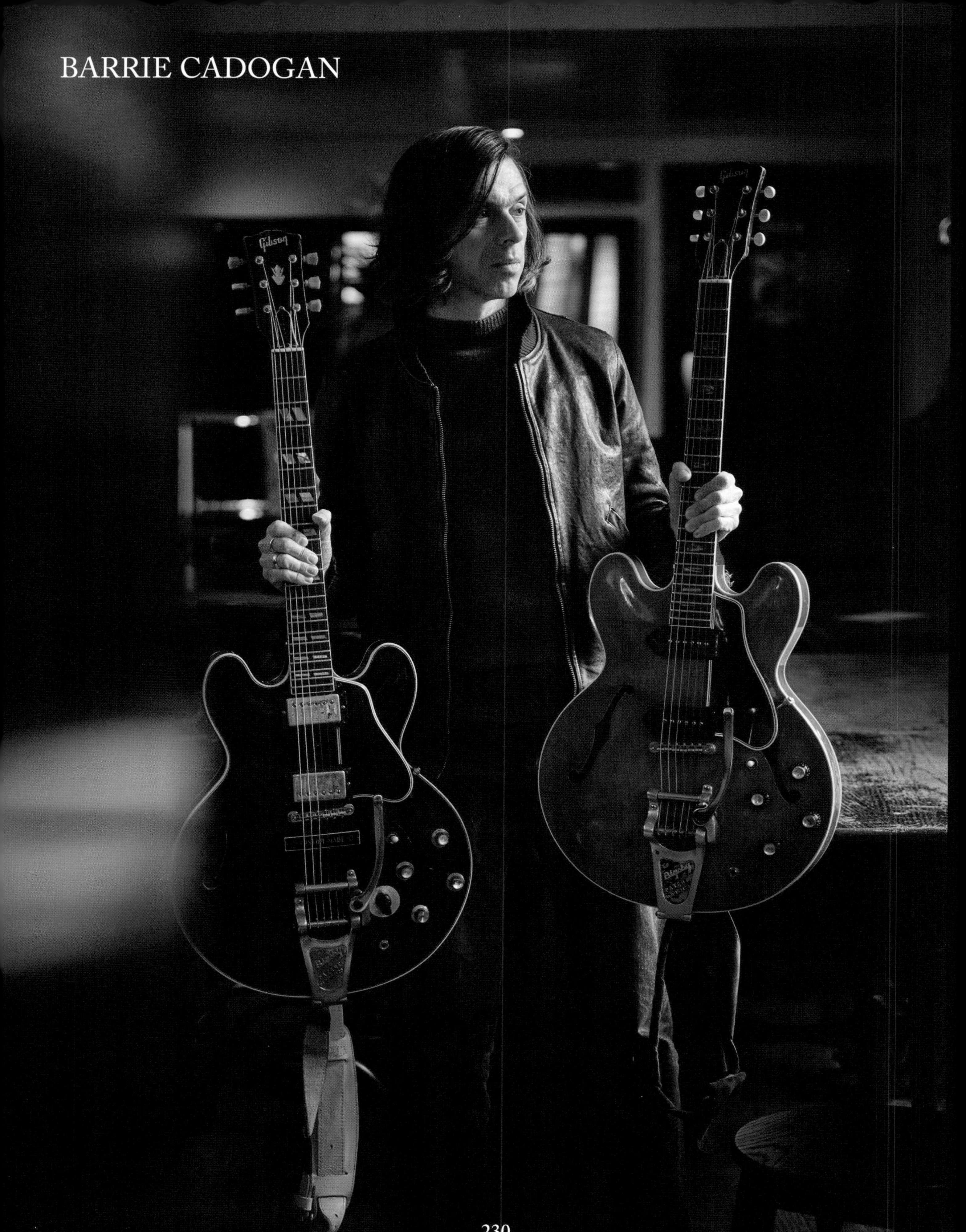

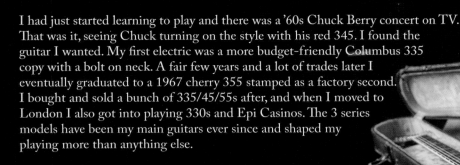

I had just started learning to play and there was a '60s Chuck Berry concert on TV. That was it, seeing Chuck turning on the style with his red 345. I found the guitar I wanted. My first electric was a more budget-friendly Columbus 335 copy with a bolt on neck. A fair few years and a lot of trades later I eventually graduated to a 1967 cherry 355 stamped as a factory second. I bought and sold a bunch of 335/45/55s after, and when I moved to London I also got into playing 330s and Epi Casinos. The 3 series models have been my main guitars ever since and shaped my playing more than anything else.

1963 Gibson ES-330 TDC Cherry
97056

I remember opening the case and first seeing this guitar. It sounds a bit daft, but I just knew it had something about it. It didn't just look good. I traded a much cleaner all original '64 330 for it which sounds even more daft. It wasn't playing its best when I got it either. It had the wrong type Bigsby fitted and a wonky setup, but it gradually just got better and better and overtook everything else. I bought the original B7 Bigsby with the weird extra drilled hole for £50 from a bloke wandering around Denmark Street with it for sale. As soon as that was installed the whole thing came alive. It became my favourite guitar and still is. It's done some miles over the years from London's 100 Club to beach festivals in Japan and sitting in with Hubert Sumlin in New York. There's been some wear and tear along the way, but it's much loved. I've learned a lot with this guitar, my playing really moved forward with it. It's been the most influential instrument on my own style and music.

Photo credit: Lee Vincent Grubb

1963 Gibson ES-345 TDSV
Refinished black over sunburst s/n 112891

I found this one after the red 330. My friend Al Duncan who worked at the shop and saved it for me without a deposit until I could get the money together. I loved the non-original black finish, which also made it more affordable. The original Bigsby had long been removed, I played it that way for several years until I bought the old B7 at Regent Sounds and the original Custom Made plate from Goodness Guitars in Tokyo. Having the wang bar back made it more versatile. It's my main session guitar. It's been around a bit, more recently at Knebworth with Liam Gallagher to The Sydney Opera House and Albert Hall with The The, plus years of touring Primal Scream and a ton of different studio jobs as well as on my own records. I also used this guitar to write and record the "Better Call Saul" theme. Thank you, Al.

Barrie

Photo credit: Lee Vincent Grubb

233

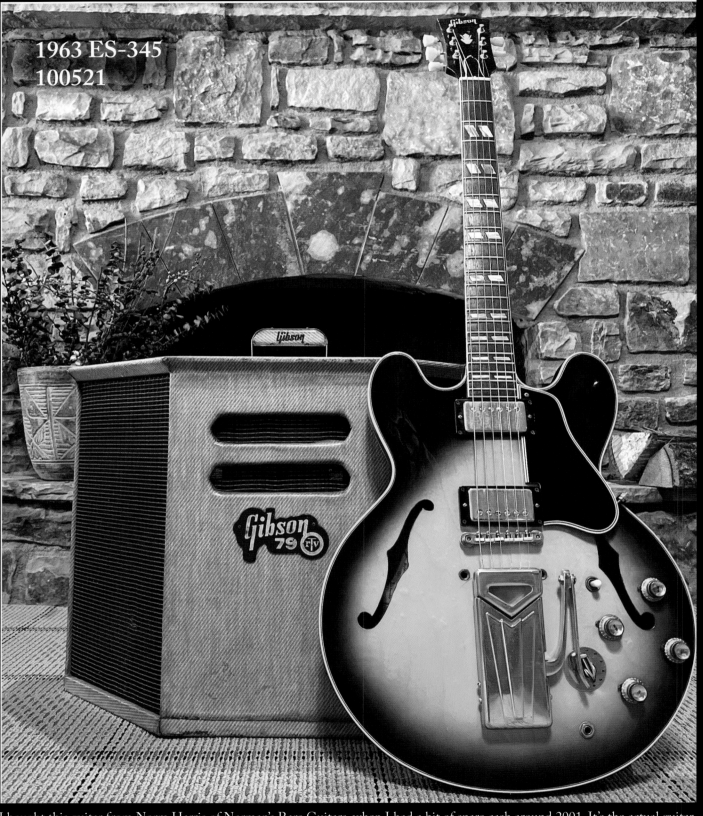

1963 ES-345
100521

I bought this guitar from Norm Harris of Norman's Rare Guitars, when I had a bit of spare cash around 2001. It's the actual guitar featured on page 170 of his collection book. It still had the original stereo lead in the case and when I plugged it into two amps in his shop it sounded like a Hammond Organ on steroids. I knew I was having it right then. "Has it got the right patent number sticker pick-ups Norm, are there any issues, do I need to take it apart?" I asked. "It's been in my warehouse for 15 years James, it's absolutely fine." I was glad I didn't take it apart in his store, when I got it home, I discovered that, unusual for a '63, it had 2 PAFs!

Quote from previous owner, James Stevenson

1963 ES-350 TDN
115563

Thanks to Andy Shapiro

1964 ES-335
66516

Thanks to Ricky Steel Edge

The Swinging Blue Jeans - Ray Ennis
1964 Gibson ES-330 TDN 158647

One of the great UK bands of the 1960s
This feature was supplied by UK vintage guitar expert Cosmo, who once owned this guitar

Ray Ennis, appearing with the band on *Top of the Pops*

1964 ES-355 TDC (mono)
179029

1964 ES-335 TDC - Special Bigsby
158721

Photo credit: Albert Molinaro

241

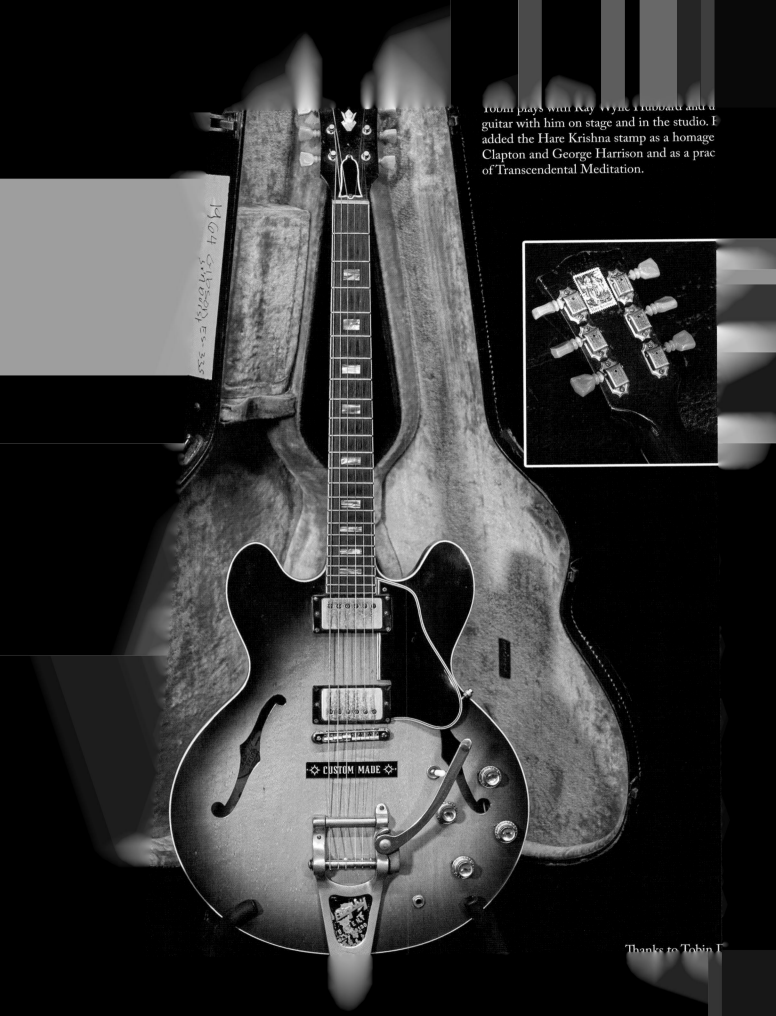

Tobin plays with Ray Wylie Hubbard and a
guitar with him on stage and in the studio. H
added the Hare Krishna stamp as a homage
Clapton and George Harrison and as a prac
of Transcendental Meditation.

1964 GIBSON ES-335

CUSTOM MADE

Thanks to Tobin I

1964 ES-330 TDC

Photo credit: Raul Barrios

STEVE HOWE

Steve Howe of Yes at the Orpheum Theater on November 9, 2022 in Madison, Wisconsin

I was turned on to the 175 D after seeing the guitar on a Wes Montgomery album cover, the whole visual aspect of the guitar appealed to me. Charing Cross road in the West End of London was a magnet for musicians and it was the famous store Selmer's which finally ordered my 175 D. This was the perfect tool for my style of playing, and became part of me throughout my career. I would use many instruments over the years, but always returned to the guitar which was part of my soul.

Steve

1964 ES-175 owned by Steve Howe. Photo courtesy Tony Bacon from the book *The Steve Howe Guitar Collection*

1964 ES-335 TDS
70653

Photo credit: Albert Molinaro

Gene Cornish: Rock and Roll Legend and Hall of Fame member

I started to have an interest in music when I was very young. I got a set of drums for Christmas but because of the noise, my career as a drummer was short-lived. My Dad then bought me an Arthur Godfrey uke. I figured out a few chords on it and became interested in guitar. I then purchased a black and gold Harmony hollow body. I played that for a while and then got a Fender duo sonic. I learned quickly on that guitar. I was a big Duane Eddy fan so in the early 60's I bought an orange Gretsch 6120. When The Beatles hit, I followed George Harrison and bought a Gretsch Country Gentleman. Unfortunately, that guitar was stolen. At this point, The Rascals were becoming very popular, and I was given an endorsement with Guild with the help of Manny's Music. I was playing an Ampeg amp with two 15 inch speakers at the time. In my guitar quest, I purchased a cherry sunburst Gibson Barney Kessel. This guitar was seen on our early TV appearances. After that, I purchased two more Gibson Barney Kessels I had made in black with a Bigsby tailpiece and L 5 necks. These were also seen on many of our live performances. I didn't stop there. I then purchased a Gibson Byrdland. I was then approached by Standel amps which I was given an endorsement.

The Rascals formed in February of 1965 and our first hit was " Good Lovin." I kept on buying guitars. I bought a Gibson SG Standard and a 1968 Les Paul Custom. I played the Les Paul Custom on "People Gotta Be Free." I also had a Gibson electric 12-string I played on "Wonderful." I used the Byrdland on "Beautiful Morning." Back then, strings were quite heavy. Gibson Sonomatic 012's are what I was using. I was a James Burton fan, and learned if you took away the low E string and moved the other strings up and replaced the high E string with a banjo string everything became easier to play and bend strings. Felix and I still tour, and I absolutely love it. These days I'm playing a Fernandes Strat with a maple neck and Seymour Duncan pickups. I now use D'addario .009 to .046 string guage. Gene has recently published a book called "Good Lovin." It has to do with his life and being a member in The Rascals.

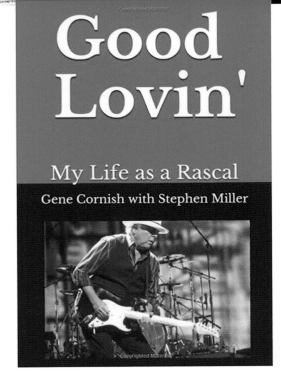

Gibson
Barney Kessel
Custom
Model

249

Alvin Lee (1944 - 2013)
ES-335 "Big Red"

Thanks to Pat Foley for this feature - Pat was responsible for the Gibson Big Red "artist" model.
It was Pat's photograph that Alvin chose for the record cover.

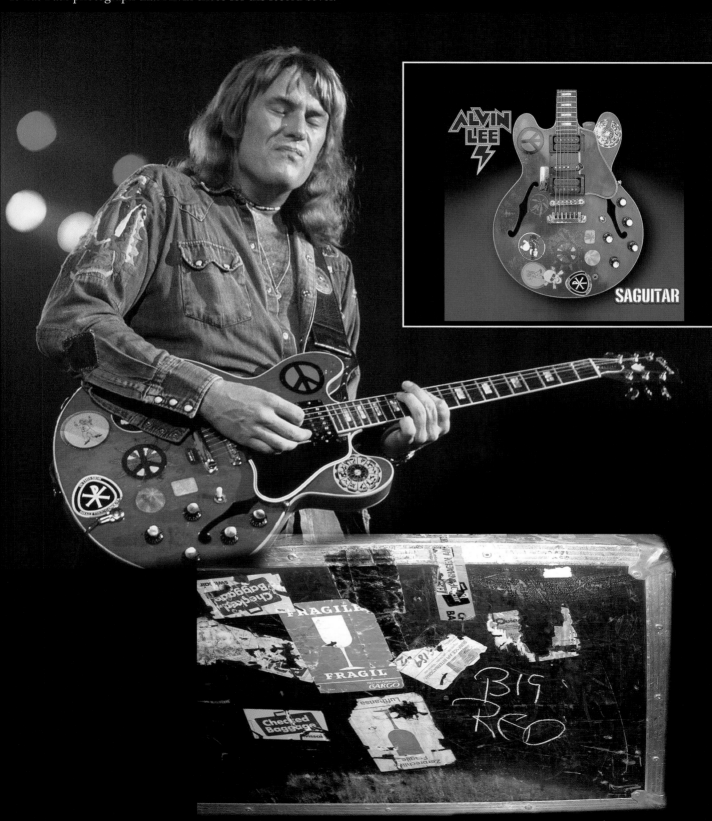

1964 ES-330 TD

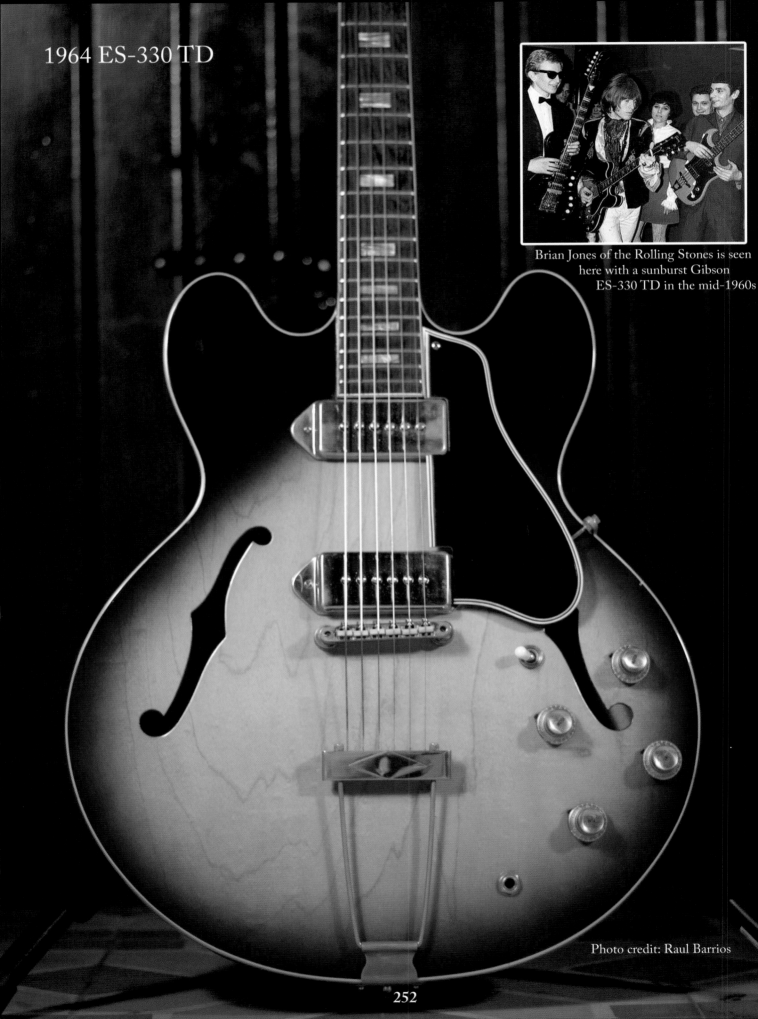

Brian Jones of the Rolling Stones is seen
here with a sunburst Gibson
ES-330 TD in the mid-1960s

Photo credit: Raul Barrios

1964 ES-330 TDC

ERIC CLAPTON

I saw a Freddy King instrumental album and he was playing a Gibson ES-335 which made it acceptable on every front - it was a Rock and Blues guitar. Guitars like the Les Paul or the ES-335 would have been the focus of my work for a long period of time - I loved the fact the "humbucker" pickups would feedback harmonically and, according to where your fingers were and where you were standing, you could control it.

The 335 was played regularly over the years and has never really changed, never getting old, wearing down or losing anything. I kept coming back to it due to nostalgia plus, anything that had been that long in my life commanded that kind of respect.

Eric

Eric Clapton performs at Madison Square Garden on
October 8, 1994 in New York City.
(Photo by Kevin Mazur/Getty Images)

Although Eric Clapton is known for his work as a Gibson Les Paul Sunburst player with the John Mayall Blues Band and the Fender Stratocaster later in his career, he is also held in high regard as a proponent of the Gibson ES 335. Eric began using an ES 335 with The Yardbirds, Cream, and Blind Faith, but it's the live recording of the song "Crossroads" by Cream that has left a huge impact on the guitar world to this day. It's one of the best live performances ever recorded with blistering guitar solos done on his ES 335. He also used this guitar on the song "Badge" and other tracks at IBC Studios in London in December 1968. Eric purchased the famed 335 from Jerry Donahue at The Selmer Store in Charing Cross Road in November of 1968. The guitar was sold by Eric at Christie's Auction House in 2004 for the amount of $847,500.

1964 ES 335 TDC
67473

Crossroads Guitar Festival - Day One
1964 Gibson ES-335TDC Crossroads Guitar Collection
Eric Clapton and friends for the Crossroads Center
(Photo by Jun Sato/WireImage)

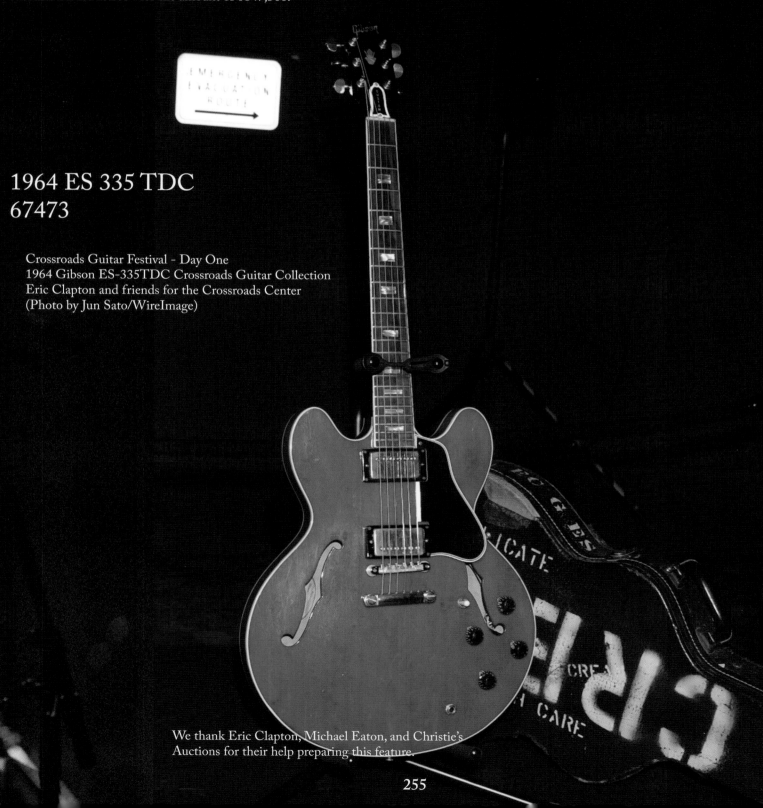

We thank Eric Clapton, Michael Eaton, and Christie's Auctions for their help preparing this feature.

1964 Cherry ES-335
67728

Photo credit: Dave Keeling

1964 Sunburst EB2
67270

John Entwistle with EB 2 Bass

257

1964 ES-335
70708

A superb example complete with stock
Maestro Vibrola

Thanks to Rick Hogue and Nick Bedessem
Garrett Park Guitars

Owned by Brent Coleman, photographed by Derek Bruneau

This 1965 ES-335 is owned by Keith Gregory who has 35 years in the vintage guitar business. Keith has worked at Gruhn Guitars and is currently with Rumbleseat Music.

Thanks to Keith Gregory

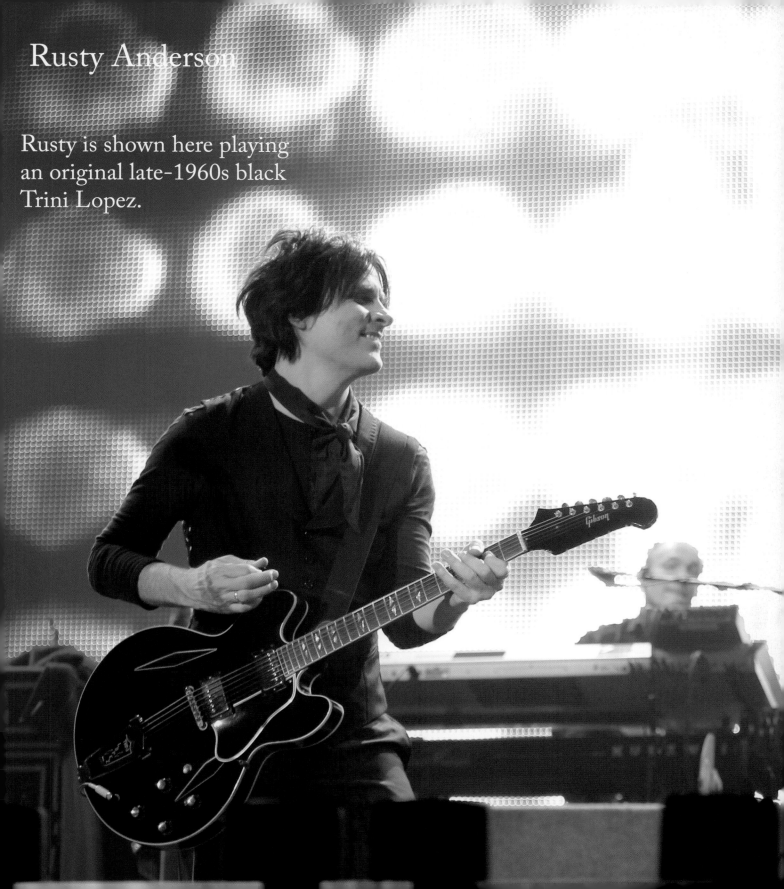

Rusty Anderson

Rusty is shown here playing an original late-1960s black Trini Lopez.

MICK MOODY - WHITESNAKE

The guitar is a true piece of British Rock and Roll history and was owned by Whitesnake's guitarist Micky Moody. The guitar has seen heavy playing and perhaps not a "case queen" - it was used as a musical instrument.

Photo credit: GuitarPoint

Thanks to Leon Windelband for this feature

1965 ES-355 TDN
307606

Thanks to Hiroshi Inoue for this feature
Guitar Licks, Kenji Hasegawa

1965 ES-125 DC
353881

Here's an ultra-rare deep body ES 125

Photo credit: Albert Molinaro

1965 Trini Lopez Model
359859

CUSTOM MADE

TRINI
LOPEZ
MODEL

Thanks to Simon Gauf
GuitarPoint

1965 Trini Lopez
359311

1969 ES-340 TDW
810517

Photo credit: George Marcinko

1966 ES-355 TDC
346387

Dave Brewis

It nails that old Eric tone. I found the guitar via an advert in Exchage & Mart in the London area

CliveWisbey

1963 ES 335
142469

This Trini has a somewhat figured top

1966 ES-345
851478
Factory Bigsby

Thanks to Andy Cesarini

1968 ES-335 12 string
530828

THE ES GALLERY

1968 ES-335 Sparkling Burgundy - Gary's Classic Guitars

1967 Trini Lopez
Standard 868383
Michael Zaporozhets

1960 ES-330
R 6773 26
Wennan Sun

1967 Gibson ES-335 TD   1963 Gibson ES-330 TD
Sunburst   Iced Tea Sunburst
907894   65955

Photo credit: Re-Caster Collection

1964 Gibson Byrdland
87395

Photo credit: Bill Townsend

ES 150 T(Tenor)

Bernie
Marsden

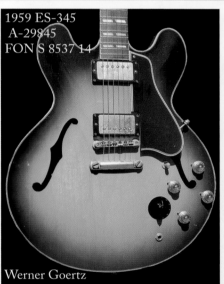

1959 ES-345
A-29845
FON S 8537 14

Werner Goertz

1966 ES-345
851478

Andy Cesarini

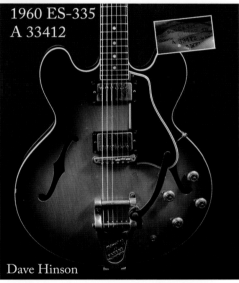

1960 ES-335
A 33412

Dave Hinson

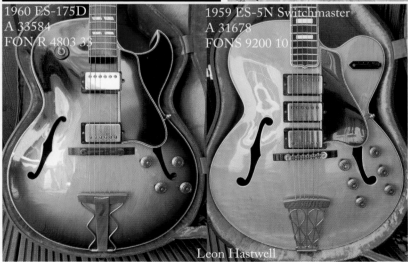

1960 ES-175D   1959 ES-5N Switchmaster
A 33584   A 31678
FON R 4803 33   FON S 9200 10

Leon Hastwell

1958 ES 335 T   A 28098
Because most unbound 335s had such shallow neck angles, Gibson
had to make a special low-profile ABR-1 for them. This one had
the normal Tune-o-matic. -*Tom Wittrock*

277

1959 ES-175 D
A32401

1959 ES-330 TD
FON
S 2801 06

1959 ES-335
A 30171

1959 ES-355TD
A 32298

Martin Lavallée

1961 A33233
An extremely hard to find
ES 355 in mono.
A pair of rare lefty guitars

1960 ES-335
2092 "R" FON

Daniel Valledor - Guitar Giraffe

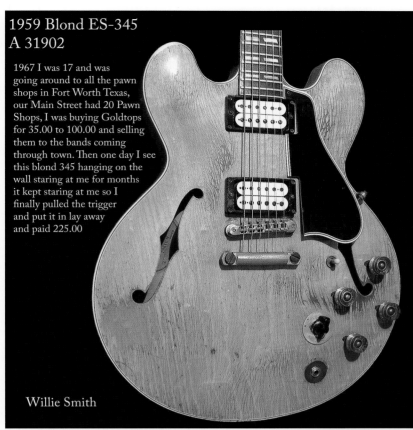

**1959 Blond ES-345
A 31902**

1967 I was 17 and was going around to all the pawn shops in Fort Worth Texas, our Main Street had 20 Pawn Shops, I was buying Goldtops for 35.00 to 100.00 and selling them to the bands coming through town. Then one day I see this blond 345 hanging on the wall staring at me for months it kept staring at me so I finally pulled the trigger and put it in lay away and paid 225.00

Willie Smith

**1959 ES-335
A 29974**

Jan Zander

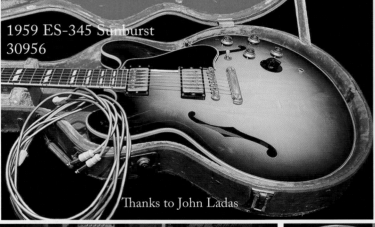

**1959 ES-345 Sunburst
30956**

Thanks to John Ladas

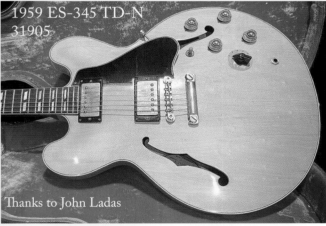

**1959 ES-345 TD-N
31905**

Thanks to John Ladas

Hiroshi Inoue
1968 ES-335   960384   951857 "Birdsong"

**1963 ES-175DN
137054**

**1959 ES-335 TDN
A 31574**

From The Thomas Tull Collection

1966-1968 with
no "F" holes -
Albert Molinaro

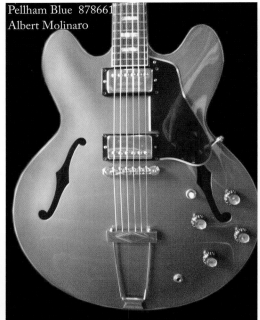

Pellham Blue 878661
Albert Molinaro

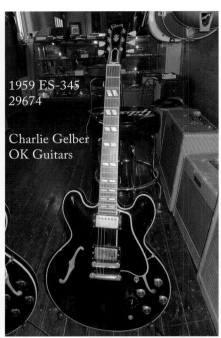

1959 ES-345
29674

Charlie Gelber
OK Guitars

1958 ES-335
A 28766
T6474-13

1958 ES-335
A28624

Elton Ko

Dag Luyten

1959 Gibson ES-355 TDSV   A 30461
factory special order stoptail 355   TJ Smith

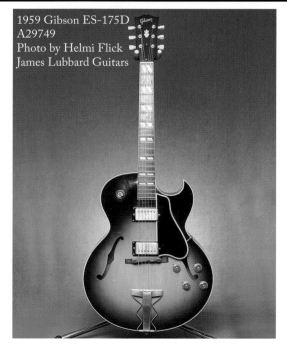

1959 Gibson ES-175D
A29749
Photo by Helmi Flick
James Lubbard Guitars

1961 ES-345
17116

1969 ES-335
818901

1964 ES-355
174687

The John Shannon Collection

280

1958 ES-335 A28752 T6473-13   Elton Ko

1962 ES-335 TDC
Dot Neck by
Helmi Flick

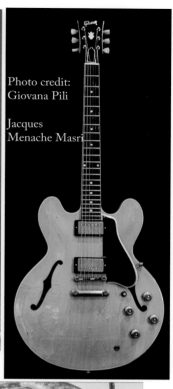

Photo credit:
Giovana Pili

Jacques
Menache Masri

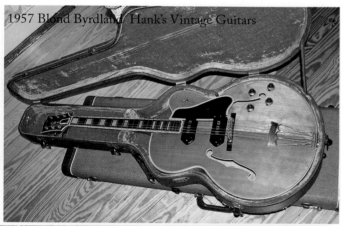

1957 Blond Byrdland Hank's Vintage Guitars

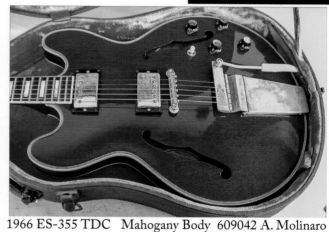

1966 ES-355 TDC   Mahogany Body 609042 A. Molinaro

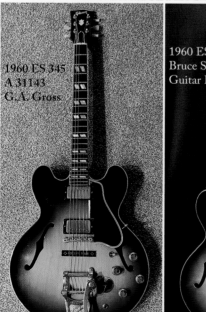

1960 ES 345
A 31143
G. A. Gross

1960 ES-335
Bruce Sandler
Guitar Exchange

1956 ES-175 A 23258
Bernie Marsden

1959 ES 225 T
James Michael Lubbard

1959 ES-335
A31555

1959 Blond 335
A 31167

1960 ES-335
Cherry Watermelon

Dave Hinson

Dave Hinson

Hiroshi Inoue

Roberto Gandolfi

1960 ES-335 A35538   1960 ES-345 A34184   1960 ES-335   A33497

1939 ES-150
Charlie Christian
EGE-5502A

1951 ES-125
7058 2

Amedeo Riccioni

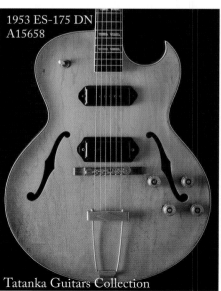

1953 ES-175 DN
A15658

Tatanka Guitars Collection

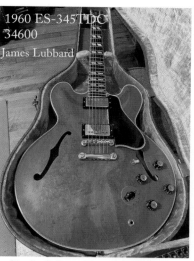

1960 ES-345TDC
34600
James Lubbard

1953 ES-295, A-15181:
One of 2 known Left Handed 53-58

1964 ES-335 TD 67818 early
1964 the same 67xxx range as EC's

1960 ES-345 TD A-33701
Early'60, possibly the earliest
Left Handed ES-345.

Charlie Gelber sold it to Geddy Lee
Geddy Lee consigned it to Mecum
Auctions I purchased it from the
Milwaukee Guitar Collective

Andy Cesarini
1960 ES-330: early 1960 '59 specs and factory Bigsby
1959 ES-345 A 31388, heavily flamed top,
1959 ES-335 A 30260, thin top, double white PAFs,
added Bigsby. Rare run of '59s with '58 specs.

1959 ES-355 mono 29556
Ruamratchata Rujinarong

1953 ES 175
Miraldo Vidal

1952 ES-350   A 10438. This guitar originally would have had P90s as well as a
dual-volume master tone control layout. The guitar was sent back to Gibson in
1964 where it was fitted with PAFs, harness, tuners.   TJ Smith

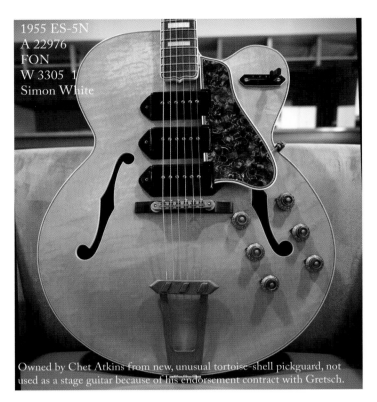

1955 ES-5N
A 22976
FON
W 3305 1
Simon White

Owned by Chet Atkins from new, unusual tortoise-shell pickguard, not used as a stage guitar because of his endorsement contract with Gretsch.

1972/3 a special order ES-175 62880. Finished in custom color golden mist poly with Super 400 inlays, ebony fingerboard and a two-piece maple neck.
Joel Peter Willing

1964 ES-345 66330
Thanks to Robbie Bergeron

1960 ES 345 A 33145
still wired in stereo. Tobi Kunze

1957 ES-175D with a 56 FON (1st week of 57 pots, very early PAF guitar) It is currently cherry red, which gets a lot of attention. It is marked as blonde in the Gibson ledger, I've heard it was a possible 60's factory refin, but I cannot confirm, the finish is definitely old though. Unfortunately, it was parted out before I got it, currently working on bringing it back with as many era correct parts as possible. *Zac Oswald*

1959 A28952
Zebra PAFs
from Andy Watts

1964 ES-335
157946
Paul Drennan

1958 ES-355
A 28413

This is the first
ES-355 built
by Gibson in
1958.
Thanks to
Brad Dudley

1962 ES-175 TDN
A 85878

1959
ES-175 TDN
A 29382

1959 ES-335TN
A 30852

Francesco Ballosino

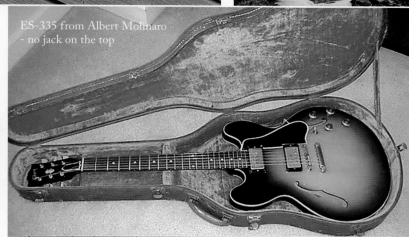

ES-335 from Albert Molinaro
- no jack on the top

1959 ES-175
A 29880

Alex Pavchinski

1959 Black ES-345 John Ladas

Taking us out, Mr. Rock 'n' Roll,
Keith Richards keeps us all
smiling and is the epitome of
ROCK.

Final Thanks

Thanks to all the friends who submitted photos and features for this edition. We were aiming for about 200 pages, but gradually increased this as it became apparent we had underestimated the number of great guitars in circulation and the support coming from our readers.

Burst Believers VI set a new standard for excellence and this volume has maintained that quality with some outstanding photographs and interesting information on these superb instruments. We have paid tribute to the early electrics and the jazz guitars and artists who morphed into the Rock 'n' Roll era. The ES guitars were a major part of the explosion into the Blues and Rock years of the 1960s, and are still loved by the guitar community.

We can't say it often enough, but thank you all for your dedication in helping us create this book. If we have missed or had to leave out any of your submissions, please understand we had the difficult choice of choosing the finest and most interesting guitars.

As always,
Keep Rocking

Vic and David

ES Believers

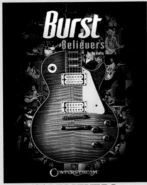 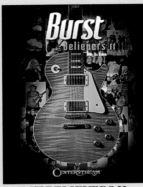 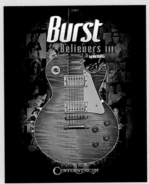
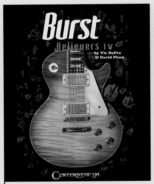  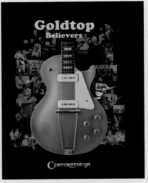
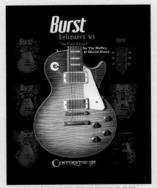